**HOW TO FIND WHAT
YOU'RE NOT LOOKING FOR**

HIDDEN
TREASURE

Discover The True
Purpose of Living

Rida Lester

Table of Contents

PART 1 5

Chapter 1: Never Give Up – 3 Reasons to Carry on Believing in Yourself During Dark Times 6

Chapter 2: How To Rid Yourself of Distraction 10

Chapter 3: *How to Value Being Alone* 13

Chapter 4: How to Deal with Stress Head On? 7 Things You Can Start Today 17

Chapter 5: How To Set Smart Goals 23

Chapter 6: Happy People Are Proactive About Relationships 26

Chapter 7: *Avoid The Dreaded Burnout* 29

Chapter 8: *Don't Let Eating, Sleeping, and Working Out Get In The Way of Your Productivity* 32

Chapter 9: **Start Working On Your Dreams Today** 35

Chapter 10: *5 Ways To Focus on Creating Positive Actions* 40

PART 2 45

Chapter 1: 5 Ways To Adopt Right Attitude For Success 46

Chapter 2: 10 habits of Beyoncé 51

Conclusion 54

Chapter 3: Happy People Do What Matters to Them 55

Chapter 4: *Five Habits of A Healthy Lifestyle* 58

Chapter 5: How to Acknowledge The Unhappy Moments? 62

Chapter 6: Distraction Is Robbing You 67

Chapter 7: 10 Habits of Mariah Carey 74

Chapter 8: The Power of Developing Eye Contact with Your Client .. 78

Chapter 9: *The Daily Routine Experts for Peak Productivity* 84

Chapter 10: Constraints Make You Better: Why the Right Limitations Boost Performance 87

PART 3 93

Chapter 1: Believe in Yourself 94

Chapter 2: Happy People Only Focus on What Is Within Their Control 96

Chapter 3: Happy People Live Slow 99

Chapter 4: 8 Ways To Deal With Setbacks In Life 106

Chapter 5: Happy People Create Time to Do What They Love Every Day 113

Chapter 6: Happy People Live Slow 116

Chapter 7: 7 Ways Your Behaviors Are Holding You Back 118

Chapter 8: 8 Habits That Can Make You Happy 123

Chapter 9: *7 Ways To Attract Happiness* 128

Chapter 10: 7 Ways To Cultivate Emotions That Will Lead You To Greatness 132

PART 1

Chapter 1:

<u>Never Give Up – 3 Reasons to Carry on Believing in Yourself During Dark Times</u>

We all have black moments. Sometimes these stretch into days, weeks and even months. Both small and huge problems can quickly overwhelm us. There are many reasons.

When we are really down, it may begin to feel like we are living a lifetime of hell. We get caught up in a swirling torrent of negativity. Light and hope fade. Emotionally and psychologically, we become spent. At the extreme, we might even begin to tell ourselves that we will never achieve success, happiness and joy ever again.

Avoiding sinking deeper and deeper into an unpleasant pit of despair can be avoided!

You need to recognize tipping points quickly. It is our cue to stop! Before you go down this rabbit hole, get proper perspective. The sooner the better. Think about it:

1. Stop Focusing Predominantly on Others

Do you still primarily look for external validation? Constantly worrying. For example, what your father wanted you to become? What he thinks of you because you flunked out of university? What he is going to say now when he hears your boss said you are the worst sales performer this month! His views on you facing the horrible prospect of unemployment? Everyone sees things differently. Actually, accepting we have very little control of what others think, feel and do is helpful. Making paramount what we think, feel and do about our life's direction and quality makes all the different. By doing this we no longer need anyone else's stamp of approval.

When we stop seeking others validation, we start seeking an authentic life. It suddenly becomes uniquely ours. Self-endorsement also feels good. Giving ourselves permission to take charge and chart our own course offers a sense of freedom. We begin to see clearly that at the end of the day, we are the best judges of our lives. It can become well lived on our terms. Let go of the rest.

2. Stop Believing Things Will Not Change

Past regrets aside, recognize you are in the here and now. Without that university degree you are never going to be that doctor your father wanted! However, you do have new options every moment. Seeing new and even creative opportunities during difficulties is the ultimate determinant of your ability to bounce back, turn things around and pursue a brighter future. Short of being fired or dying, there is still time to become the top sales person. It depends if you want it enough.

Think about the different periods, people and situations in your life. Each of us is living proof of constant change. We certainly can't stop the cycle of change. Our only option is really how we respond to the constant flow. Growth and progress are about making the most of change including obstacles and challenges. Often, we will deny the inevitability of change in an attempt to try avoid confronting our worst fears. We may fail. Again, and yet again. We need to find the courage to go for it irrespective. Committing to the idea that embracing change gives us another opportunity to get better and learn. Current results are temporary and stepping stones.

3. Stop Not Seeing Your Worth

When important people in our lives tell us that we are not good enough, it can be earth shattering. When we tell ourselves, we are not good enough, this is outright dangerous. Especially so if we are astute enough to know that the most significant opinion in our life is our own. Any lack of self-worth limits potential to come out undamaged from dark periods. We can get over the bosses' views that we will never cut it as a high-flying sales guru. But it becomes impossible to lift ourselves up and see the light when we forget our own brilliance and essence. We must self-affirm to create self-love. We need to know our worth even when others miss it.

It is a crucial part of life's journey to find one's true self. This can mean deciding to change a sales career at any point, including to that of a life as a nomad. We need to make choices that maximize our sense of self-worth, not erode it. There is no prescribe perfect life trajectory. Once we can measure ourselves as much for our internal achievements, as by our external achievements in the world, we would have found hidden treasure. Self-worth is the cornerstone of mental health and stability. Block by block we can build this foundation as a fortress against any and all negative onslaughts that come our way.

So, if we remain focused on these 3 important thoughts, we will strengthen our innate ability to survive whatever life throws our way. Resilience becomes our armor as we conquer our demons. Whatever shape or size they may appear in. We are ready.

Chapter 2:
How To Rid Yourself of Distraction

Distraction and disaster sound rather similar.
It is a worldwide disorder that you are probably suffering from.
Distraction is robbing you of precious time during the day.
Distraction is robbing you of time that you should be working on your goals.
If you don't rid yourself of distraction, you are in big trouble.

It is a phenomenon that most employees are only productive 3 out of 8 hours at the office.
If you could half your distractions, you could double your productivity.
How far are you willing to go to combat distraction?
How badly do you want to achieve proper time management?

If you know you only have an hour a day to work, would it help keep you focused?

Always focus on your initial reason for doing work in the first place.
After all that reason is still there until you reach your goal.

Create a schedule for your day to keep you from getting distracted.
Distractions are everywhere.
It pops up on your phone.
It pops up from people wanting to chat at work.
It pops up in the form of personal problems.
Whatever it may be, distractions are abound.

Hidden Treasure

The only cure is clear concentration.
To have clear concentration it must be something you are excited about.
To have clear knowledge that this action will lead you to something exciting.

If you find the work boring, It will be difficult for you to concentrate too long.
Sometimes it takes reassessing your life and admitting your work is boring for you to consider a change in direction.

Your goal will have more than one path.
Some paths boring, some paths dangerous, some paths redundant, and some paths magical.
You may not know better until you try.
After all the journey is everything.

If reaching your goal takes decades of work that makes you miserable, is it really worth it?
The changes to your personality may be irreversible.

Always keep the goal in mind whilst searching for an enjoyable path to attain it.
After all if you are easily distracted from your goal, then do you really want it?

Ask yourself the hard questions.
Is this something you really want? Or is this something society wants for you?

Many people who appear successful to society are secretly miserable.
Make sure you are aware of every little detail of your life.
Sit down and really decide what will make you happy at the end of your life.

What work will you be really happy to do?

What are the causes and people you would be happy to serve?

How much money you want?

What kind of relationships you want?

If you can build a clear vision of this life for you, distractions will become irrelevant. Irrelevant because nothing will be able to distract you from your perfect vision.

Is what you are doing right now moving you towards that life?

If not stop, and start doing the things what will.

It really is that simple.

Anyone who is distracted for too long from the task in hand has no business doing that task. They should instead be doing something that makes them happy.

We can't be happy all the time otherwise we wouldn't be able to recognize it.

But distraction is a clear indicator you may not be on the right path for you.

Clearly define your path and distraction will be powerless.

Chapter 3:
How to Value Being Alone

Some people are naturally happy alone. But for others, being solo is a challenge. If you fall into the latter group, there are ways to become more comfortable with being alone (yes, even if you're a hardcore extrovert).

Regardless of how you feel about being alone, building a good relationship with yourself is a worthy investment. After all, you *do* spend quite a bit of time with yourself, so you might as well learn to enjoy it.

Being alone isn't the same as being lonely.

Before getting into the different ways to find happiness in being alone, it's important to untangle these two concepts: being alone and being lonely. While there's some overlap between them, they're completely different concepts. Maybe you're a person who basks in solitude. You're not antisocial, friendless, or loveless. You're just quite content with alone time. You look forward to it. That's simply being alone, not being lonely.

On the other hand, maybe you're surrounded by family and friends but not relating beyond a surface level, which has you feeling empty and disconnected. Or maybe being alone just leaves you sad and longing for company. That's loneliness.

Short-term tips to get you started

These tips are aimed at helping you get the ball rolling. They might not transform your life overnight, but they can help you get more comfortable with being alone.

Some of them may be exactly what you needed to hear. Others may not make sense to you. Use them as stepping-stones. Add to them and shape them along the way to suit your lifestyle and personality.

1. **Avoid comparing yourself to others.**

This is easier said than done, but try to avoid comparing your social life to anyone else's. It's not the number of friends you have or the frequency of your social outings that matters. It's what works for you.

Remember, you have no way of knowing if someone with many friends and a stuffed social calendar is happy.

2. Take a step back from social media.

Social media isn't inherently bad or problematic, but if scrolling through your feeds makes you feel left out and stresses, take a few steps back. That feed doesn't tell the whole story. Not by a long shot.

You have no idea if those people are truly happy or just giving the impression that they are. Either way, it's no reflection on you. So, take a <u>deep breath</u> and put it in perspective.

Perform a test run and ban yourself from social media for 48 hours. If that makes a difference, try giving yourself a daily limit of 10 to 15 minutes and stick to it.

Don't be afraid to ask for help.

Sometimes, all the self-care, exercise, and gratitude lists in the world aren't enough to shake feelings of sadness or loneliness.

Consider reaching out to a therapist if:

- You're overly <u>stressed</u> and finding it difficult to cope.
- You have <u>symptoms of anxiety</u>.
- You have <u>symptoms of depression</u>.

You don't have to wait for a crisis point to get into therapy. Simply wanting to get better and spending time alone is a perfectly good reason to make an appointment.

Chapter 4:

How to Deal with Stress Head On? 7 Things You Can Start Today

Drop your shoulders, release your tongue from your palate. Unclench your teeth and let your brows relax. You see, this is how stressed you are all the time, you forget completely about how it is affecting your body.

In this roaring river of the 21st century, we are all feeling the tide rising and falling 24/7. It will be a white lie if any of you claim to never feel stressed. We are all under varying degrees of stress all the time.

So what is stress exactly? Stress is not merely a stimulus or a physical response of our bodies but a process by which we appraise and cope with environmental threats and challenges. When expressed in short bursts or taken as a challenge, stressors may have positive effects. However, if stress is threatening or prolonged, it can be harmful for us.

So how then do we handle it?

It seems like quite a drag for most of us and pretty annoying a lot of the time, but here are several ways we can deal with it and come out of it stronger than before.

7 Tips to Deal with stress and anxiety

Number 1: Go To Bed Early and Wake up Early

Have you heard the quote "Early to Bed, early to rise, makes a man healthy, wealthy and wise."? When was the last time you went to sleep early? I believe that going to bed early is something we all know we need to do but hardly ever do.

Starting your day off early has many wonderful biological effects. Mornings tend to be cool, silent, serene, and distraction-free. This calmness helps bring our stress levels down and prepares us for the day ahead. By practicing some deep breathing techniques in the morning, it will also aid in flow and circulation throughout our bodies, something that is good for the mind and soul.

Number 2: Start Practicing Yoga or meditation

Yoga and meditation, while they are two separate practices, they overlap in many key areas. Yoga poses are great for us to engage with our bodies, to stretch out our muscles, tight sections of our bodies, and to help us focus on our breath at all times. Each yoga pose targets a unique meridian of our bodies, many allowing us to release tensions that might otherwise have built up without realizing. You can try simple poses such as a child pose or shavasana, or downward dog, to get yourself started.

Meditation on the other hand focuses stilling the mind through focus on the breath as well. Letting our thoughts flow freely, we are able to acknowledge the stressors we face without judgement. Try out some guided mindfulness meditation practices to get your started.

Number 3: Having Proper Time Management

Many of us overlook the importance of proper time management. We often let our crazy schedules overwhelm us. By being unorganized with our time, we are also unorganized with our emotions. If we let our calendar be filled with chaos, there is no doubt that we will feel like chaos as well. Stress levels will be bound to rise. Have proper blocks of time dedicated to each task in your day. Trust me you will feel a whole lot more in control of everything.

Number 4: Make time for your hobbies

We should all strive to live a happy and balanced life. If work is the only thing on our agenda, we will have no outlet to destress, relax, recharge, and be ready to face new challenges that might tax our physical and mental abilities.

Whatever your hobbies are: baking, tennis, crafting, surfboarding, or even shopping, as long as you plan them in your schedule and do them, you will definitely feel a whole lot better about everything. Let out all the steam, stress, anxieties, as you engage in your hobbies, or even just forget about them for a minute. Give yourself the space to breathe and just enjoy doing the fun things in life. Life isn't just all about work. Play is equally important too.

Number 5: Music is food for your soul

Music has many therapeutic qualities. If you feel your stress levels rising, consider popping your earbuds into your ears and playing your favorite songs on spotify. If you are looking for calm, you may want to consider listening to some chill music as well.

The kind of your music you listen to will have a direct effect on your mood and the way you feel. So choose your playlists wisely. Don't go heavy metal or goth, unless of course it helps calm you down.

Number 6: Start Cleaning your clutter

This may seem like I am quoting a movie where the stressed teenage girl decides to clean her room when she is feeling low. I'd say movies are made out of someone's real experience.

Cleaning your room or clutter can be one of the best therapies.

A messy space is a recipe for anxiety and stress. When we see clutter, we feel cluttered. Once you clear all the stuff you don't need, you will feel much lighter instantly.

Number 7: Allow nature to heal you

Nature is amusing and wonderful. Everything in nature is closer to our basic making than anything that we are dealing with today. So try getting close to nature, it will make you feel relaxed and at the same time enable you to enrich your brain.

Watch the sun setting into the sky and wake up to look at the colors at dawn.
There is nothing more beautiful in this world that we get to experience every single day no matter where we are on this earth.

Take a stroll in your favourite park, go for a cycle, a jog, or even just a stroll with your pet. Allow nature to melt away your stress and bring your peace.

Final Thoughts

Stressors are a part of life. Something we cannot escape from. But if we put in place some healthy habits and practices, we can reduce and release those negativities from our bodies, cleansing us to take on more stress in the future.

Chapter 5:

How To Set Smart Goals

Setting your goals can be a tough choice. It's all about putting your priorities in such a way that you know what comes first for you. It's imperative to be goal-oriented to set positive goals for your present and future. You should be aware of your criteria for setting your goals. Make sure your plan is attainable in a proper time frame to get a good set of goals to be achieved in your time. You would need hard work and a good mindset for setting goals. Few components can help a person reach their destination. Control what you choose because it will eternally impact your life.

To set a goal to your priority, you need to know what exactly you want. In other words, be specific. Be specific in what matters to you and your goal. Make sure that you know your fair share of details about your idea, and then start working on it once you have set your mind to it. Get a clear vision of what your goal is. Get a clear idea of your objective. It is essential to give a specification to your plan to set it according to your needs.

Make sure you measure your goals. As in, calculate the profit or loss. Measure the risks you are taking and the benefits you can gain from them.

In simple words, you need to quantify your goals to know what order to set them into. It makes you visualize the amount of time it will take or the energy to reach the finish line. That way, you can calculate your goals and their details. You need to set your mind on the positive technical growth of your goal. That is an essential step to take to put yourself to the next goal as soon as possible.

If you get your hopes high from the start, it may be possible that you will meet with disappointment along the way. So, it would be best if you made sure that your goals are realistic and achievable. Make sure your goal is within reach. That is the reality check you need to force in your mind that is your goal even attainable? Just make sure it is, and everything will go as planned. It doesn't mean to set small goals. There is a difference between big goals and unrealistic goals. Make sure to limit your romantic goals, or else you will never be satisfied with your achievement.

Be very serious when setting your goals, especially if they are long-term goals. They can impact your life in one way or another. It depends on you how you take it. Make sure your goals are relevant. So, that you can gain real benefit from your goals. Have your fair share of profits from your hard work and make it count. Always remember why the goal matters to you. Once you get the fundamental idea of why you need this goal to be achieved, you can look onto a bigger picture in the frame. If it doesn't feel relevant, then there is no reason for you to continue working for. Leave it as it is if it doesn't give you what you applied for because it will only drain your energy and won't give you a satisfactory outcome.

Time is an essential thing to keep in focus when working toward your goals. You don't want to keep working on one thing for too long or too short. So, keep a deadline. Keep a limit on when to work on your goal. If it's worth it, give it your good timer, but if not, then don't even waste a second on it. They are just some factors to set your goals for a better future. These visionary goals will help you get through most of the achievements you want to get done with.

Chapter 6:
Happy People Are Proactive About Relationships

Researchers have found that as human beings we are only capable of maintaining up to 150 meaningful relationships, including five primary, close relationships.

This holds true even with the illusion of thousands of "friends" on social media platforms such as Facebook, Instagram, and Twitter. If you think carefully about your real interactions with people, you'll find the five close/150 extended relationships rule holds true.

Perhaps not coincidentally, Tony Robbins, the personal development expert, and others argue that your attitudes, behavior, and success in life are the sum total of your five closest relationships. So, toxic relationships, toxic life.

With this in mind, it's essential to continue to develop relationships that are positive and beneficial. **But in today's distracted world, these relationships won't just happen.**

We need to be proactive about developing our relationships.

My current favorite book on personal development is Tim Ferriss's excellent, though long, 700+ page book, *Tools of Titans: The Tactics, Routines, and Habits of Billionaires, Icons, and World-Class Performers*.

At one point, Ferriss quotes retired women's volleyball great Gabby Reece:

I always say that I'll go first.... That means if I'm checking out at the store, I'll say "hello" first. If I'm coming across somebody and make eye contact, I'll smile first. [I wish] people would experiment with that in their life a little bit: be first, because — not all times, but most times — it comes in your favor... The response is pretty amazing.... I was at the park the other day with the kids.

Oh, my God. Hurricane Harbor [water park]. It's like hell. There were these two women a little bit older than me. We couldn't be more different, right? And I walked by them, and I just looked at them and smiled. The smile came to their face so instantly. They're ready, but you have to go first because now we're being trained in this world [to opt out] — nobody's going first anymore.

Be proactive: start the conversation

I agree. I was excited to read this principle because I adopted this by default years ago, and it's given me the opportunity to hear the most amazing stories and develop the greatest relationships you can imagine.

On airplanes, in the grocery store, at lunch, I've started conversations that led to trading heartfelt stories, becoming friends, or doing business together. A relationship has to start someplace, and that can be any place in any moment.

Be proactive: lose your fear of being rejected
I also love this idea because it will help overcome one of the main issues I hear from my training and coaching clients – the fear of making an initial connection with someone they don't know.

This fear runs deep for many people and may be hardwired in humans. We are always observing strangers to determine if we can trust them – whether they have positive or dangerous intent.

In addition, **we fear rejection. Our usual negative self-talk says something like,** *If I start the conversation, if I make eye contact, if I smile, what if it's not returned?*

What if I'm rejected, embarrassed, or ignored by no response? I'll feel like an idiot, a needy loser.

Chapter 7:
Avoid The Dreaded Burnout

Do you often lack the energy to get on with any new task and feel sluggish throughout most of your day? Do you feel the burden of work that keeps getting pilled up each day?

I know we all try our best to manage everything on our hands and try to bring out the best in us. But while doing so, we engage in too many things and ultimately they take their toll.

It is becoming easier and easier every day where people have more work than ever on their hands. And their sole motive throughout life becomes, to find more and better ways of earning a better living. To find more things to be good and successful at.

We all have things on our hands to complete but let me tell you one thing. You won't be able to continue much longer if you keep with this burnout and exhaustion.

Our body is an engine and it needs a way of cooling down and tuning. So what's the first step you need to reduce burnout? You need to get the right amount of sleep.

There is this myth that you sleep one-third of your life so you don't need an 8-hour sleep. You can easily do the same with four hours and use the other four for more work. Trust me, this is not a myth, it is a misconception about proven research. Your body organs deserve at least half the time of what they spend serving us.

We can refresh and better our focus and cognitive skills once we have a good night's sleep full of dreams.

Another thing that most of us avoid doing is to say No to anyone anytime. The thing is that we don't have any obligation to anyone unless we are bound by a contract of blood or law to do or say anything that anyone tells us to do. The more we feel obligated to anyone, the more we try to do to impress that person or entity with our efforts and conduct.

This attitude isn't healthy for any relation. Excess of anything has never brought any good to anyone. So don't give up everything on just one thing. Instead, try to devise a balance between things. Over-commitment is never a good idea.

The third and final thing I want you to do is to give up on certain things at certain times. You don't need to carry your phone or laptop with you all day. This only creates a distraction even when you don't need to be in that environment.

You don't need to train your subconscious to be always alert on your emails and notifications or any incoming calls all day long. But sometimes you just need to give up on these things and zone out of your repetitive daily life.

Doing your best doesn't always mean giving yourself all out. Sometimes the best productive thing you can do is to relax. And that, my friends, can help you climb every mountain without ever getting tired of trying t do the same trail.

Chapter 8:

Don't Let Eating, Sleeping, and Working Out Get In The Way of Your Productivity

From the time of Man's descend on this planet, We have literally been eating, sleeping, and working for our basic requirements.

With time and population, we did invent some things which were perfected with time as well. But in general, when you leave your teenage or enter middle age, you get into this routine of chores that only keep the cycle of life running.

The things that we take for granted today, were considered magic only a couple of hundred years ago. The feats we have done in the last fifty years may be more important and revolutionary compared to all human history. But this hasn't stopped us from seeking more.

We have two basic requirements to live; We need air to breathe and we need food to fuel up the tank. But if we start to live our lives only for those two things alone, we are no better than a prehistoric caveman.

The purpose of life is far bigger than what we perceive today.

Yeah, sometimes we get into existential crisis because we never really know what our lives mean. What the future will be and can be? What will happen at the end of all this? What was our purpose all along?

These things are natural to every sane human perception and thinking. Some people spend all their lives in search of the true meaning, in search of the truth. But the truth is that you can never know even if you have all things planned with a foolproof sketch.

But what I can tell you is that no effort goes to waste if you have a true motive. We have come too far to give up on things and leave them for others to complete. We can be satisfied with living a simple life of straightforward tasks, but we can never be fully content with our lives.

Human nature dictates us to have a second look, a second thought on even the most obvious things around us. This habit of questioning everything has brought us out of the supernatural and made us achieve things that were not even in the realm of magic.

The biggest hunger a human mind can have is the hunger for knowledge. Human beings were meant to shape up the world for the better.

Human consciousness is so vast that its limits are still unknown. So why are we still stuck on the same habits and knowledge we were born with. Why can't we ask more questions? Why can't we try to find more answers?

The only way forward for us is to keep feeding ourselves more goals and more reasons to get busy.

Life isn't just about getting up in the morning. It is about finding our true potential. It is about finding easier ways to solve problems. It is about finding bigger, better, and greater things for the generations to come.

We were given this life to inspire and be inspired. But if we have nothing new to offer to at least ourselves, what purpose are we serving then?

Chapter 9:
Start Working On Your Dreams Today

When did you get up today? What was your day like? What did you achieve today? Did any of that matter?

Maybe it didn't because you don't have any dreams to work towards, or maybe that you've forgotten what they are altogether.

To have a dream is to have a direction in life. To have a dream means you have something bigger than yourself that you want to achieve.

Everyone gets at least one chance in their life to actually go and pursue that dream, but few recognize that until it is too late. It is too late to regret when you are on your deathbed wondering what could have been. That is when it is too late to work on your dreams. When you have no more time left.

The Moment to start working On your dreams is right here right now.

We repeat our failures every day but never learn. We get depressed every day but never communicate. We get bullied every day, but never fight back. Why?

Is it because we can't do it? No, Definitely Not! We can do it whenever we want. We can do it today. We can do it the next minute. We just lack Ambition!

Every day someone achieves something big. Some more than often, others maybe not their whole life. But the outcome is **not** determined by **fate**, but with **Effort**.

All the billionaires you see today started out with a few dollars just like you and me. They just had the guts to pursue their dream no matter what the cost is. They all had a vision of something bigger. They went full throttle even when everyone around them expected them to fail. Even when they met with struggles that hit them harder than the last, they were still focused on the dream. Never did they once lesson the effort.

No two persons are born the same. Not the same face, color, intelligence, or fate. But what's common for every human being is the built-in trait to strive for a goal once they are determined enough. Doesn't matter if it's food for the next meal or success for the times to come.

The struggle is real, it always was, it always will be. The world wouldn't be what it is today if it weren't for the struggle man has gone through over the centuries. The struggle is the most real definition of life in this world. But that doesn't mean it's a bad one.

Our parents struggled to make us a better person. They put in their best effort to watch us succeed in our dreams. Their parents did the same for them and their parents before them.

This is what makes life a cycle of inherited struggle and hardships. Nobody asks to struggle through a hard life, but we can all turn the hard life into a meaningful one. The life that we all should expect to eventually achieve only if we keep the cycle running and if we keep putting in the effort.

How then do we actually work towards our dreams? By focusing on the things that matter each and every day, again and again, until that mountain has been conquered. Don't forget to enjoy the journey, because it could well be the best part of the trip up top.

You never know what the next moment has in it for you. You can never predict the future, but you can always hope for a better one. You only get the right to hope if you did what was meant to be done today. It's your lawful right to reap the fruit if you took care of sowing the seeds faithfully and diligently all through the year.

The motivation behind this continuous grind of time in search of that Dream lies in your past. You cannot achieve those dreams until you start treasuring the lessons of your past and become a person who is always willing to go beyond.

You can't simply depend on hope to get something done. You have to reach the point where start obsessing over that goal, that thing, that DREAM. When you start obsessing, you start working, you start seeing the possibilities and you just keep going. If you don't get up then you WILL miss the moment. The moment that could have made all the difference in the world. If you don't act upon that impulse, you might never get that inspiration ever again. And that will be the moment you will always regret for the rest of your life.

Remember that your whole life is built on millions of tiny decisions. A decision to just act on one of those moments can transform your life completely. These moments often test you too. But only for an inch more before you find eternal glory. So don't wait for someone else to do it for you. Get up, buckle up, and start doing. Because only you Can!

Chapter 10:

5 Ways To Focus on Creating Positive Actions

Only a positive person can lead a healthy life. Imagine waking up every day feeling like you are ready to face the day's challenges and you are filled with hope about life. That is something an optimist doesn't have to imagine because they already feel it every day. Also, scientifically, it is proven that optimistic people have a lower chance of dying because of a stress-caused disease. Although positive thinking will not magically vanish all your problems, it will make them seem more manageable and somewhat not a big deal.

All you have to do is focus on the positive side of life. It is not necessarily true that people with a positive mindset always get disappointed. Positivity is like a breath of fresh air for us. Looking at the bright side of things has its advantages, and it has its very own benefits. So, positive energy is an essential factor to produce in oneself to make them more efficient in the ways of life. They tend to focus on all the good things and push aside all the wrong things, making them love everything they do.

1. **Think Positively**

Positive thinking is what leads to positive actions, actions that affect you and the people around you. When you think positively, your actions show how positive you are. You can create positive thinking by focusing on the good in life, even if it may feel tiny thing to feel happy about because when you once learn to be satisfied with minor things, you would think that you no longer feel the same amount of stress as before and now you would feel freer. This positive attitude will always find the good in everything, and life would seem much easier than before. You then become the person you once imagined yourself to be, just by thinking positively about it. So, make sure to process those positive thoughts thoroughly for better results or action.

2. Be Grateful

Being grateful for the things you have contributed a lot to your positive behavior. Gratitude has proven to reduce stress and improve self-esteem. Think of the things you are grateful for; for example, if someone gives you good advice, then be thankful to them, for if someone has helped you with something, then be grateful to them, by being grateful about minor things, you feel more optimistic about life, you feel that good things have always been coming to you. Studies show that making down a list of things you are grateful for during hard days helps you survive tough times. Also, be thankful to yourself for making achievements that you wanted. It makes you feel positive about yourself and makes your confidence boost through you. You have to make sure that you know what it is to be thankful for. Be grateful to someone for all the right reasons, and you will feel positive.

3. Laugh Through Situations

A person laughing always looks like a happy person. Studies have shown that laughter lowers stress, anxiety, and depression. Open yourself up to humor, permit yourself to laugh even if forced because even a forced laugh can improve your mood. Laughter lightens the mood and makes problems seem more manageable. Your laughter is contagious, and it may even enhance the perspective of the people around us. Smiling is free therapy. You have to pass an approving smile and make someone's day up.

4. Don't Blame Yourself For The Things You Can't Control

People with depression or anxiety are always their jailers; being harsh on themselves will only cause pain, negativity, and insecurity. So try to be soft with yourself, give yourself a positive talk regularly; it has proven to affect a person's actions. A positive word to yourself can influence your ability to regulate your feelings and thoughts. The positivity you carry in your brain is expressed through your actions, and who doesn't loves an optimistic person. Instead of blaming yourself, you can think differently, like "I will do better next time" or "I can fix this." Being optimistic about the complicated situation can lead your brain to find a solution to that problem.

5. **Start Your Day with A dose of Positivity**

When you wake up, it is good to do something positive in the morning, which mentally freshens you. You can start the day by reading a positive quote about life and understand the meaning of that quote, and you may feel an overwhelming feeling after letting the meaning set. Everybody loves a good song, so start by listening to a piece of music that gives you positive vibes, that gives you hope, and motivation for the day. You can also share your positivity by being nice to someone or doing something nice for someone; you will find that you feel thrilled and positive by making someone else happy.

Conclusion

Indeed, we can not just start thinking positively overnight, but we have to push ourselves more every time to improve. Surround yourself with brightness, good people, and a positive mindset—a good combination for a good life.

PART 2

Chapter 1:
5 Ways To Adopt Right Attitude For Success

Being successful is a few elements that require hard work, dedication, and a positive attitude. It requires building your resilience and having a clear idea of your future ahead. Though it might be hard to decide your life forward, a reasonable manner is something that comes naturally to those who are willing to give their all. Adopting a new attitude doesn't always mean to change yourself in a way but, it has more meaning towards changing your mindset to an instinct. That is when you get stressed or overworked is because of an opposing point of view on life.

With success comes a great sense of dealing with things. You become more professional, and you feel the need to achieve more in every aspect. Don't be afraid to be power-hungry. But, it also doesn't mean to be unfair. Try to go for a little more than before, each step ahead. Make your hard work or talent count in every aspect. Make yourself a successful person in a positive manner, so you'll find yourself making the most of yourself. And don't give up on the things you need in life.

1. **Generate Pragmatic Impressions**

"The first impression is the last impression." It's true that once you've introduced yourself to the person in front of you, there is only a tiny chance that you'll get to introduce yourself again. So, choosing the correct wording while creating an impression is a must. You need to be optimistic about yourself and inform the other person about you in a way that influences them. An impression that leaves an effect on them, so they will willingly meet you again. A person must be kind and helpful towards its inferior and respectful towards their superior. This is one of the main characteristics for a person to be a successful man or woman. And with a negative attitude, the opposite occurs. People are more inclined to work without you. They nearly never consider you to work with them and try to contact you as little as possible. So, a good impression is significant.

2. **Be True To Your Words**

Choose your wording very carefully, because once said, it can't be taken back. Also, for a successful life, commitment is always an important rule. Be true to what you said to a person. Make them believe that they can trust you comfortably. So, it would be best if you chose your words. Don't commit if you can't perform. False commitment leads to loss of customers and leads to the loss of your impression as a successful worker. Always make sure that you fulfill your commands and promises to your clients and make them satisfied with your performance. It leads to a positive mindset and a dedication to work towards your goal.

3. A Positive Personal Life

Whatever you may be doing in your professional life can impact your personal life too. Creating the right mindset professionally also helps you to keep a positive attitude at home. It allows you to go forward with the proper consultation with your heart. It will make you happier. You'll desire to achieve more in life because you'll be satisfied with your success. It will push to go furthermore. It will drive you towards the passion for desiring more. Hard work and determination will continue to be your support, and you will be content will your heart. By keeping a good attitude, you'll be helping yourself more than helping others.

4. Be Aggressive and Determined

Becoming goal-oriented is one of the main factors evolving success in your life. If you are not determined to do your work, you'll just accept things the way others present you. It will leave you in misery and deeply dissatisfied with yourself. Similarly, you'll tend to do something more your way if you are goal-oriented and not how others want. You'll want to shale everything according to your need, and you become delighted with yourself and the result of your hard work. Always keep a clear view of your next step as it will form you in to your true self. Don't just go with the flow, but try to change it according to your wants and needs.

5. Create Your Master Plan

Indeed, we can't achieve great things with only hard work. We will always need to add a factor or to in our business. But by imagining or strategizing, some plans might be helpful. With hard work and some solid projects, we will get our desired outcome. If not, at least we get something close. And if you chose the wrong option, then the amount of hard work won't matter. You'll never get what you want no matter the hard work. So, always make sure to make plans strategically.

Conclusion

By keeping a positive attitude, you'll not only be helpful to others but to yourself too. Make sure you keep the proper manner—a manner required to be a successful person. Do lots of achievements and try to prove yourself as much as possible. Try keeping a good impact on people around you in everything you do. Have the spirit and courage to achieve great heights. And be sure to make moat of yourself. Consistency is the key.

Chapter 2:
10 habits of Beyoncé

Beyonce is a renowned Houston-born singer, dancer, songwriter, actor, and businesswoman. She rose to prominence as a member of the pop singing R&B group "Destiny's Child." Beyonce is ultimately life goals; she is always at the top of her game, tries new things (and smashes them), admits her mistakes, balances her family life, and spends time with the people who matter. She always points out on working tirelessly to the top with the help of her mother and father from the age of nine.

How has she managed to win Grammys, make platinum albums, star in many A-list films, run a lucrative clothing line, perfume business, and raising three gorgeous children?

Here are 10 Mrs. Carter habits that you can emulate.

1. Above All, Love Yourself

Beyonce have had a share of work-family balance struggles when raising her three kids. Realizing how overwhelming it can be, she opts for self-love practices that means more rest if need be. You have goals and desires, which is terrific! But it's pointless making all that only to die as soon as you acquire it. Practise self-care.

2. Make the Most of Your Time

Beyonce's advice as a self-made millionaire is not to waste time. If you want to attain your goals, you must respect your time before others do. Everyone, rich or poor, has the same number of hours in a day. But the question is, what are you doing with your 24 hours? Are you making the best use of your time?

3. Keep Your Personal Life a Mystery

Talking to Oprah in an interview, "Queen Bey" said that she is purposefully private because revealing everything deprives her of enjoying her personal life. Your personal life should be sacred because letting everyone in may ruin it.
Beyonce believes that he fans should only be familiar with her through her art and music; the rest she reserves for her family and friends.

4. Love Your Body

Beyoncé is a representation of beauty, power, and health. Beyoncé recently claimed that she has been following a vegan diet, not for weight loss, but to be the best version of herself. Spending time on yourself is crucial, and learning to love yourself is imperative, whether the healthiest version of yourself means giving up meat or simply spending an extra few hours in the gym each month.

5. Be the Best Version of You

If there is one thing we can learn from Beyonce, is that no one will scold you on bringing out your best. Quoting her words in her documentary, "power will never be given to you; you must take it yourself." If you want it big, nobody is going to do it for you. If you are not invited to the table, drag yourself a chair and sit.

6. Take Charge of Your Success

Beyonce is a good example of what economic equality is. She is one who doesn't shy off celebrating her achievements as a woman. Beyonce isn't afraid to flaunt her "paper" and personal accomplishments. She is always proud of her hustle and isn't afraid to exploit her past triumphs to prove her worth. That is how you advance - both professionally and personally.

7. Hard Work Is Recognizable

A "smart person" will frequently imply that good soft skills can compensate for time spent on "the little things." However, Beyonce's stage appearance and performance demonstrates that hard work will be appreciated by those who admire your work, as well as those who don't know you.

8. Opinionated

Beyonce is defined by her beauty and brains. She is an activist on important topics, for instant, her opinions had an influence during

Obama's administration, and she also promoted Michelle Obama's efforts to promote humanitarianism. Weigh in your opinion where it matters.

9. Negativity Derails You

Stay away from negativity and concentrate on working hard and doing your best. Beyonce is a challenge to most of her peers in the industry because she does not waste time on frivolous things and the negative people on her pages trying to bring her.

10. Her Priorities

Beyoncé's story revolves around her family, and she frequently emphasizes it as her driving force. Those people who journey with you from scratch to success are the same people who you should credit.

Conclusion

There is nothing powerful than knowing and respecting your worth as well as remaining solid on your money-making journey. Even if you don't have Beyoncé's level of riches, learn to handle your life cautiously.

Chapter 3:
Happy People Do What Matters to Them

Think about what you want most out of life. What were you created for? What is your mission in life? What is your passion? You were put on this earth for a reason, and knowing that reason will help you determine your priorities.

I spent a total of four months in the hospital, healing from my sickness. During that time, I spent a lot of time thinking about my purpose in life. I discovered that my purpose is to help you change your lives by focusing on what matters most to you.

1. Create A Plan

Create a plan to get from where you are today to where you want to be. Maybe you need a new job. Maybe you need to go back to school. Maybe you need to deal with some relationship issues. Whatever it is, create a plan that will get you to where you want to be.

While I was in the hospital, I began to draft my life plan. My plan guides all of my actions, helps me focus on my relationships with my wife and daughter, and helps me keep working toward my life purpose. A life plan will help you focus your life too.

2. Focus On Now

Stop multitasking and focus on one thing at a time. It may be a project at work. It may be a conversation with your best friend. It may just be the book that you have wanted to read for months. The key is to focus on one thing at a time.

I plan each day the night before by picking the three most important tasks from my to-do list. In the morning, I focus on each one of these tasks individually until they are completed. Once I complete these three tasks, I check email, return phone calls, etc.

3. Just Say "No."

We all have too much to do and too little time. The only way you will find the time for the things that matter is to say "no" to the things that don't.

I use my purpose and life plan to make decisions about the projects and tasks I say yes to. If a project or task is not aligned with my purpose, a good fit with my life plan, and sometimes that I have time to accomplish, I say no to the project. Saying no to good opportunities gives you time to focus on the best opportunities.

Research tells us that 97 percent of people are living their life by default and not by design. They don't know where their life is headed and don't plan what they want to accomplish in life.

These steps will help you to decide what matters most to you. They will help you to begin living your life by design and not by default. Most importantly, they will help you to create a life focused on what matters to you.

Let me end by asking, "What matters most to you?

Chapter 4:
Five Habits of A Healthy Lifestyle

A healthy lifestyle is everybody's dream. The young and old, rich and poor, weak and strong, and male and female all want a happily ever after and many years full of life. The price to pay to achieve this dream is what distinguishes all these classes of people. What are you ready to forego as the opportunity cost to have a healthy lifestyle?

Here are five habits for a healthy lifestyle.

1. Eating Healthy Food

Your health is heavily dependent on your diet. You have heard that what goes inside a man does not defile him, but what goes out of him does. In this case, the opposite is true. What a man takes as food or beverage affects him directly. It can alter the body's metabolism and introduce toxins in the body hence endangering his life.

Most people do not take care of what they feed on. They eat anything edible that is readily available without any consideration. All other factors like the nutritive value of the food and its hygiene are secondary to most modern people who have thrown caution to the wind. Towns and cities are full of fast food joints and attract masses from all over. It is the most lucrative business these days. Are these fast foods healthy?

As much as the hygiene could be up to standards (due to the measures put in place by authorities), the composition of these foods (mostly chips and broiler chicken) is wanting. The cooking oil used is full of cholesterol that is a major cause of cardiac diseases. To lead a healthy lifestyle, eating healthy food should be a priority.

2. Regular Exercising

The human body requires regular exercise to be fit. Running, walking, swimming, or going to the gym are a few of the many ways that people can exercise. It is a call to get out of your comfort zone to ward off some lifestyle diseases. It is often misconstrued that exercising is a reserve for sportsmen and women. This fallacy has taken root in the minds of many people.

Unlearn the myths about exercises that have made most people shun them. The benefits of exercising are uncountable. It improves pressure and blood circulation in the body. Exercises also burn excess calories in tissues that would otherwise clog blood vessels and pose a health hazard. Research has shown that most people who exercise are healthy and fall sick less often. This is everyone's dream but the few who choose to pay the price enjoy it. Choose to be healthy by doing away with frequent motor vehicle transport and instead walk. A simple walk is an exercise already. When you fail to exercise early enough, you will be a frequent patient at the hospital. Prevention is always better than cure.

In the words of world marathon champion, Eliud Kipchoge, a running nation is a healthy nation.

3. Regular Medical Checkup

When was the last time you went for a medical checkup even when you were not sick? If the answer is negative or a long time ago, then a healthy lifestyle is still unreachable. A medical examination will reveal any disease in its early stages.

In most third-world countries, healthcare systems are not fully developed. Its citizens only go to the hospital when a disease has progressed and is in its late stages. At such a time, there is a higher probability of the patient succumbing to it. Doctors advise people to seek medical attention at the slightest symptom to treat and manage long-term illnesses. Regular medical checkups help one become more productive at work.

Is a healthy lifestyle attainable? Yes, it is when one takes the necessary measures to fight diseases. Regular medical checkups can be financially draining. Seek an insurance policy that can underwrite your health risks and this will make medical expenses affordable.

4. Staying Positive

A bad attitude is like a flat tire. If you do not change it, you will never go anywhere. There is a hidden power in having a positive attitude towards life. It all starts in the mind. When you conceive the right attitude towards life, you have won half the battle.

A healthy lifestyle starts with the mind. If you believe it, you can achieve it. So limitless is the human mind that it strongly influences the direction of a person's life. As much as there are challenges in life, do not allow them to conquer your mind or take over your spirit. Once they do, you will be constantly waging a losing battle. Is that what we want?

Associate with positive like-minded people and you will be miles away from depression and low self-esteem. We all desire that healthy lifestyle.

5. Have A Confidant And A Best Friend

Who is a best friend? He/she is someone you can trust to share your joy and sadness, and your high and low moments. You should be careful in your selection of a confidant because it may have strong ramifications if the friendship is not genuine.

A confidant is someone you can confide in comfortably without fear of him/her leaking your secrets. He/she will help you overcome some difficult situations in life. We all need a shoulder to lean on in our darkest times and a voice to comfort us that it is darkest before dawn. This helps fortify our mental health. We grow better and stronger in this healthy lifestyle.

These are the five habits for a healthy lifestyle. When we live by them, success becomes our portion.

Chapter 5:
How to Acknowledge The Unhappy Moments?

In today's video we will talk about how we can embrace the unhappiness moments in our lives and turn them into power and strength that will carry us through life gracefully.

We all have moments in life when we are not happy, we're scared, we're apprehensive, mildly depressed even, and the pain is difficult to endure. Whether it be because we have lost a friend, someone we love, or that we are simply not happy at our jobs. There could be a million reasons for our unhappiness.

In these trying times we only want an escape. To escape from our pain, our unhappy feelings because we are not ready to deal with the things that are going wrong in our lives. We don't want to acknowledge our unhappy moments because this makes us grieve and inflict more pain.

All these ways of avoiding the acknowledgment only perpetuate our feelings in long run. Avoidance only brings us misery and suffering in the long run. It keeps us from living to our fullest potential. It keeps us from the very fact that there is light at the end of the tunnel, and that we need to keep moving forward.

It is very important that you acknowledge your unhappy moments because you can only move forward with confidence once you accept that life being unhappy is simply a part of life. How can you admire happiness and the joys in your life if you have not gone through any unhappy moments? If you have nothing to compare it to?

It is not always easy to acknowledge the unhappy moments in life. But here are 5 powerful ways to help you along with the process.

Recognize the Reason of your unhappiness

First step of acknowledgment is to recognize the problem, find the real reason why you are unhappy. If, for example, you think you are not happy at your job, instead of pointing fingers at the obvious issues you are facing, ask yourself the deeper questions. Questions like, do I feel like I belong here? Do I feel I'm making a difference? Is what I am doing fulfilling my true desires? If the answer to those questions is a resounding no, it could be that your heart is, at that very moment, not in this job. You might be feeling as though you are spinning on a hamster wheel, going around in circles with nowhere in sight. It is very important to understand the true reason for your unhappiness because you cannot cut the stem and think that the tree will not grow again.

Take a moment and stop

Once you have found the problem, take a moment, and just stop right there. Don't suppress the feelings. Take a deep breath and sit with it for a while. Just sit there and be with it. Acknowledge that you have identified the essence of the unhappiness that had been festering in you for a while. And be glad that you now have something to work with to change your situation.

Accept what it is

Once you have found the root of the problem it's time to accept it. As Thick Nhat mentioned in his book "Peace is every step". He writes that it is important to mentally acknowledge our feelings. Say out loud if you feel like it, "I can accept that I am experiencing intense unhappiness right now. And that it is okay. And that I will be okay."

Once you have embraced your moments of unhappiness you can overcome the feelings and move forward with peace.

If you are embracing your moments of unhappiness, you can create a mental space and see around it instead of being enmeshed in them. This space will open new doors and help you overcome your feelings as you embrace new beginnings that will soon come your way.

Plan Next Best Move

Now that you have successfully identified the reason for your unhappiness, it is time to find out what your next best move is. In life we never really know what the next right move is, we can only hope and trust that our decisions will work for us in the end.

Take the time to write down the things you want and the things that can change your situation. Things that can potentially move you out from a place of unhappiness. Going back to the previous problem that we have discussed, if it is your job that is causing distress in your life, what are the potential ways you can apply to mitigate the problem, would it be to quit or could you find a compromise somewhere. Talking to a colleague, a friend, or even your boss to let you explore your areas of creativity and things you excel at could be a welcome change.

Whatever the potential may be, no matter how big or small, you have the power to change your situation. Don't stay trapped in that situation for too long as it will only bring you down further along the road.

Believe Things Will Work Out In The End

Hope is a very powerful thing. Now that we have a plan, we need to have faith and just believe that our actions will pay off. We can never predict the future, and so taking one step at a time is the best thing we can do. We have to believe that whatever we are doing to change our situation will turn our unhappiness around sooner or later.

Final Thoughts

Happy and unhappy moments are part of life, like day and night, light, and darkness.

If you only believe in one thing, believe that change is the only constant and that bad times don't last forever. You will be happy again and you will move forward gracefully. And this is only possible if acknowledge your unhappy moments.

Happiness Is just right around the corner.

Chapter 6:
Distraction Is Robbing You

Every second you spend doing something that is not moving you towards your goal, you are robbing yourself of precious time.
Stop being distracted!

You have something you need to do,
but for some reason become distracted by
other less important tasks and procrastinate on the important stuff.
Most people do it,
whether it's notification s on your phone or chat with colleges,
mostly less than half the working day is productive.

Distraction can be avoided by having a schedule
which should include some down time to relax
or perhaps get some of them distractions out of the way,
but time limited.

As long as everything has its correct time in
your day you can keep distraction from stealing too much of your time.
When your mind is distracted it becomes nearly impossible to
concentrate on the necessary work at hand.

Always keep this question in mind:
"is what I am about to do moving me towards my goal?"
If not, is it necessary?
What could I do instead that will?

It's all about your 24 hours.
Your actions and the reactions to your actions from that day,
good or bad.
By keeping your mind focused on your schedule that
moves you towards your goal, you will become resilient to distraction.

Distraction is anything that is not on your schedule.
You may need to alter that depending on the importance of the intrusion.
Being successful means becoming single minded about your goal.
Those with faith do not need a plan b because they know plan A is the only way and they refuse to accept anything else.

Any time you spend contemplating failure will add to its chances of happening.
Why not focus on what will happen if you succeed instead?

Distraction from your vision of success is one of its biggest threats.
Blocking out distraction and keeping that vision clear is key.
Put that phone on flight mode and turn off the TV.

Focus on the truly important stuff.

If you don't do it, it will never get done.
The responsibility is all yours for everything in your life.
The responsibility is yours to block out the distractions and exercise your free-will over your thoughts and actions.

By taking responsibility and control you will become empowered.
Refuse to let anyone distract you when you're working.
Have a set time in your schedule to deal with stuff not on the schedule.
This will allow you time to deal with unexpected issues without stopping you doing the original work.
The reality is that we all only have so much time.
Do you really want to waste yours on distractions?
Do you want to not hit your target because of them?
Every time you stop for a notification on your phone you are losing time from your success.
Don't let distraction rob you of another second, minute, hour or day.
Days turn to months and months turn to years don't waste time on distractions and fears.

Six Habits of The Mega-Rich

There are rich people then there are the mega-rich. The distinction between them is as clear as day. The former are still accumulating their wealth while the latter is beyond that. Their focus is no longer on themselves but humanity. Their view of things is through the prism of business and not employment. Their business enterprises are well established and their level of competition is unmatched. They are at the top of the pyramid and have a clear view of things below.
Here are six habits of the mega-rich:

1. They Have a Diversified Investment Portfolio

The mega-rich are ardent followers of the saying "do not put all your eggs in one basket." They have stakes in every type of business across many world economies beginning with their country. Their patriotism makes them not leave out their countries when they do business.
With diversified risk across various sectors of the economy, they can remain afloat even during tough economic times. Their companies and businesses also yield high returns because of proper management and their diversification.

2. They Are Generous

The mega-rich people are generous to a fault. They run foundations and non-governmental organizations in their name with a cause to help humanity. It indicates their generosity and desire to help the most vulnerable and needy in society. Generosity is a hard trait to trace these days and it distinguishes the mega-rich from kind people.

The generosity of mega-rich people seeks to help the needy permanently by showing them how to fish instead of giving them fish. Such an act liberates families from poverty and promises a brighter future to the younger generation.

3. They Are Neither Petty Nor Trivial

Pettiness is not the character of mega-rich people. They do not have time for small squabbles and fights. Instead, they use their energy in pursuit of more productive goals. Their minds always think of their next big move and ways to improve their businesses. They do not have time to engage in non-issues.

Mega-rich investors do not undertake trivial investments. Their businesses are major leaving people marveling at its grandiose. Jeff Benzos took a trip to space and the world was amazed. The impact the ilk of Benzos has in the world economy is unmatched; securities exchanges and global trade shakes whenever such people make a business move.

4. They Have A Clean Public Image

The mega-rich people manage to maintain a scandalous-free public image. This is crucial for their success. When was the last time you came across a character-damaging story of a wealthy person? It is difficult to recall. Perception tends to stick in the minds of people more than reality. This makes it important for them to guard their reputation with their life. If you are on the path of joining the exclusive club of the mega-rich, begin cleaning up your reputation if it is a mess. Build a new public image that will portray you as a better person to the world. Mega-rich people intimidate by their angel-like reputations and immense influence on their social status.

5. They Have Great Character

A man's character precedes his reputation. Every wealthy person upgrades his/hers. The mega-rich treasure character too much because they are unable to buy it at any price. It is invaluable. Characterlessness is a type of poverty only curable the hard way. There is no shortcut to it except tireless and intentional channeling of your efforts to strengthen it. A great character is an asset envied by the great and mighty because most of them fall short of it. There are untold stories of the efforts mega-rich people put to build their character. This has formed part of their routine and life habit.

6. They Champion Global Causes

Mega-rich people are champions of social justice and world causes like climate change and global warming. They give their contribution towards global causes without any self-interest. They are at the forefront offering support in whatever capacity.

They invest in these worthy causes because of the duty of corporate social responsibility they owe the world. It is not a debt they pay but an act they do gladly because they have the best interest of the world at heart.

These six habits of the mega-rich have formed their lifestyle. Walk in their footsteps if you want to become like them. You will command respect from everybody. Your business moves shall determine world market trends and you shall set the pace in every sector of the economy.

Chapter 7:
10 Habits of Mariah Carey

Mariah Carey has earned not only a "diva" reputation but also a legendary pop icon for over 30 years in the spotlight. She's an American singer-songwriter, actress, and record producer who has lauded her as a "songbird supreme" and the "queen of Christmas." Despite a challenging start, her debut album charted no. 1 in the US, went multi-platinum, and earned her Grammy Awards for Best Female Vocalist and Best Artist.

She is one of the most successful female performers of all time, with more than 200 million albums sales landing her a net worth of $320 million. Her distinctive acute euphonies and melismatic runs continues shaping pop music up to date. If you're wondering how this simple New York girl climbed up to becoming this legendary, this is for you!

Here are the ten habits of Mariah Carey.

1. Made the Most of What She Was Good At

According to Mariah Carey, she discovered her singing strengths at the age of 6 when her friend, whom she was singing with while holding hands, surprisingly stopped to listen to her. It was from this moment she realized that she had something exceptional and devoted to it. Knowing your strength and devoting entirely to it will eventually land you a lucky spot.

2. Leave No Doubt

Taking your game to the next level can be daunting, and it takes confidence to do so. Mariah Carey's career began magically, but it wasn't long before trolls and haters sprouted. Trolls accused her of being "studio warm" because her voice was so flawless, to be true. She was so troubled by such critics that she decided to shock her detractors with a live performance on MTV.

3. Passion Never Goes Wrong

When Mariah decided to ditch her pop image to focus on R&B and Hip Hop, her decision, as she mentioned in an interview, did not sit well with her record label at first. But eventually resulted to a breakthrough album that is still regarded as the best to date. That's what happens when you believe in your abilities and take a stand for them. Simply put, you're the one who knows how far your abilities can stretch.

4. Forget Plan B, Go Hard on Plan A

To meet your success, you need one well-thought-out plan. With a well-organized plan, make decisions that are in line with your ultimate success objectives. Mariah Carey's music was her life and she was serious and ambitious. Go all in and carry out your only plan as if your life depended on it.

5. Persistence

Perseverance, not talent, is the secret to success. "I knew in my heart that one day I'd make it... Every day that I made it through, I knew I was getting closer to my goal. "Every night, I would thank God for the day when I didn't give up or be knocked down," Carey said in an interview. When you are ambitious, pushing hard is core to achieving your goals.

6. She's All About Equality

If you have a platform, use it to propel influence against societal injustices. Carey received the GLAAD Ally Award in 2016 for her support of the LGBT community. She once assisted one of her backup dancers in proposing to his boyfriend on stage. According to GLAAD CEO Sarah Kate, Mariah Carey has always inspired and encouraged numerous LGBT admirers worldwide with her unwavering commitment to acceptance and inclusive campaigns.

7. A Little Downtime Won't Harm

Mariah mentioned her prior husband's mental and emotional abuse, as well as the chaotic filming of Glitter, in an interview. She worked 22 hours a day, which harmed her mental health and led to her hospitalization in 2001. Your lofty goals demand a healthy mind and body.

8. Explore Constantly

Allow yourself to make mistakes and explore without feeling obligated to deliver a saleable piece every time. Because of Mariah's daring explorations, Male-female collaborative raps and melodies were created by hip hop artists. There's a lot more, but the bottom takeaway is that Maria Carey's daring approach to music paid off.

9. Dream Big

You don't need to know how you'll accomplish the tremendous success you want for yourself; all you need to know is that it will happen. Carey envisioned herself taking off the music industry without doubt and also surpassing Joan Crawford's manor's splendour.

10. Follow Your Superiors

If opportunities don't come knocking at your door, make a door. When Mariah first started recording demos in high school, she met older and more experienced musicians than her. And boy, did she learn! It's also where she worked with Brenda K. Starr, a Puerto Rican freestyle singer. It was through the star that she got noticed by big bosses.

Conclusion

Of course, you don't need to follow suit completely, but you can learn from the divas herself that faith, desire, perseverance, and how serious you take your dreams important manifestation tools.

Chapter 8: The Power of Developing Eye Contact with Your Client

We've all heard the age-old saying the "eyes are the window to the soul," and in many ways, it holds. Everybody knows looking others in the eyes is beneficial in communication, but how important is eye contact, and how is it defined?

Eye contact can be subtle or even obvious. It can be a glaring scowl when a person is upset or a long glance when we see something off about someone else's appearance. It can even be a direct look when we are trying to express a crucial idea.

1) Respect

In Western countries like the United States, eye contact is critical to show and earn respect. From talking to your boss on the job or thanking your mom for dinner, eye contact shows the other person that you feel equal in importance.

There are other ways to show respect, but our eyes reflect our sincerity, warmth, and honesty.

This is why giving and receiving eye contact while talking is a surefire sign of a good conversation. Nowadays, it's common for people to glance at their phones no matter if they're in the middle of a conversation or not. That's why eye contact will set you apart and truly show that you give them your full and undivided attention.

2) Understanding

Sometimes locking glances is the only sign you need to show someone that you understand what they are talking about. More specifically, if you need to get a vital point across, eye contact is the best way to communicate that importance. Eye contact is also a form of background acknowledgment like saying "yeah" and "mhmm."
That means it shows the speaker that you are tuned in to and understand what they are saying.

3) Bonding

When someone is feeling an emotion or just performing a task, the same neurons that shine in their brain light up in someone else's brain who is watching them. This is because we have "mirror neurons" in our brains that are very sensitive to facial expressions and, most importantly, eye contact.

Direct eye contact is so powerful that it increases empathy and links together emotional states. Never underestimate the power of eye contact in creating long-lasting bonds.

4) Reveal Thoughts and Feelings

We have countless ways of describing eyes, including "shifty-eyed," "kind-eyed," "bright-eyed," "glazed over," and more. It's no wonder just about every classic love story starts with "two pairs of eyes meeting across the room." Eye contact is also a powerful form of simultaneous communication, meaning you don't have to take turns doing the communicating.

Ever wonder why poker players often wear sunglasses inside? It's because "the eyes don't lie." We instinctually look into people's eyes from birth to try and understand what they are thinking, and we continue to do it for life.

Never Give Up – 3 Reasons to Carry on Believing in Yourself During Dark Times

We all have black moments. Sometimes these stretch into days, weeks and even months. Both small and huge problems can quickly overwhelm us. There are many reasons.

When we are really down, it may begin to feel like we are living a lifetime of hell. We get caught up in a swirling torrent of negativity. Light and hope fade. Emotionally and psychologically, we become spent. At the extreme, we might even begin to tell ourselves that we will never achieve success, happiness and joy ever again.

Avoiding sinking deeper and deeper into an unpleasant pit of despair can be avoided!

You need to recognize tipping points quickly. It is our cue to stop! Before you go down this rabbit hole, get proper perspective. The sooner the better. Think about it:

1. Stop Focusing Predominantly on Others

Do you still primarily look for external validation? Constantly worrying. For example, what your father wanted you to become? What he thinks of you because you flunked out of university? What he is going to say now when he hears your boss said you are the worst sales performer this month! His views on you facing the horrible prospect of unemployment? Everyone sees things differently. Actually, accepting we have very little control of what others think, feel and do is helpful. Making paramount what we think, feel and do about our life's direction and quality makes all the different. By doing this we no longer need anyone else's stamp of approval.

When we stop seeking others validation, we start seeking an authentic life. It suddenly becomes uniquely ours. Self-endorsement also feels good. Giving ourselves permission to take charge and chart our own course offers a sense of freedom. We begin to see clearly that at the end of the day, we are the best judges of our lives. It can become well lived on our terms. Let go of the rest.

2. Stop Believing Things Will Not Change

Past regrets aside, recognize you are in the here and now. Without that university degree you are never going to be that doctor your father wanted! However, you do have new options every moment. Seeing new and even creative opportunities during difficulties is the ultimate determinant of your ability to bounce back, turn things around and pursue a brighter future. Short of being fired or dying, there is still time to become the top sales person. It depends if you want it enough.

Think about the different periods, people and situations in your life. Each of us is living proof of constant change. We certainly can't stop the cycle of change. Our only option is really how we respond to the constant flow. Growth and progress are about making the most of change including obstacles and challenges. Often, we will deny the inevitability of change in an attempt to try avoid confronting our worst fears. We may fail. Again, and yet again. We need to find the courage to go for it irrespective. Committing to the idea that embracing change gives us another opportunity to get better and learn. Current results are temporary and stepping stones.

3.   Stop Not Seeing Your Worth

When important people in our lives tell us that we are not good enough, it can be earth shattering. When we tell ourselves, we are not good enough, this is outright dangerous. Especially so if we are astute enough to know that the most significant opinion in our life is our own. Any lack of self-worth limits potential to come out undamaged from dark periods. We can get over the bosses' views that we will never cut it as a high-flying sales guru. But it becomes impossible to lift ourselves up and see the light when we forget our own brilliance and essence. We must self-affirm to create self-love. We need to know our worth even when others miss it.

It is a crucial part of life's journey to find one's true self. This can mean deciding to change a sales career at any point, including to that of a life as a nomad. We need to make choices that maximize our sense of self-worth, not erode it. There is no prescribe perfect life trajectory. Once we can measure ourselves as much for our internal achievements, as by our external achievements in the world, we would have found hidden treasure. Self-worth is the cornerstone of mental health and stability. Block by block we can build this foundation as a fortress against any and all negative onslaughts that come our way.

So, if we remain focused on these 3 important thoughts, we will strengthen our innate ability to survive whatever life throws our way. Resilience becomes our armor as we conquer our demons. Whatever shape or size they may appear in. We are ready.

Chapter 9:
The Daily Routine Experts for Peak Productivity

What is the one thing we want to get done for a successful life? That is an effective daily routine to go through the day, every day. History is presented as an example that every high achiever has had a good routine for their day. Some simple changes in our life can change the outcome drastically. We have to take the experts' advice for a good lifestyle. We have to choose everything, from color to college, ourselves. But an expert's advice gives us confidence in our choice.

You have to set the bar high so that you get your product at the end of the day. Experts got their peak productivity by shaping their routine in such a way that it satisfies them. The productivity expert Tim Ferriss gave us a piece of simple yet effective advice for such an outcome. He taught us the importance of controlling oneself and how essential it is to provide yourself with a non-reactive practice. When you know how to control yourself, life gets more manageable, as it gives you the power to prevent many things. It reduces stress which gets your productivity out.

Another productive expert of ours, Cal Newport, gives us his share of information. He is always advising people to push themselves to their limits. He got successful by giving his deep work more priority than other work. He is managing multitasks at the same time while being a husband and a father. He is a true example of a good routine that leads to positive productivity. It would help if you decided what matters to you the most and need to focus on that. Get your priorities straight and work toward those goals. Construct your goals and have a clear idea of what your next step will be. It will result in increasing your confidence.

Now, the questions linger that how to start your day? Early is the answer. Early to bed and early to rising has been the motto of productive people. As Dan Ariely said, there is a must 3 hours in our day when our productivity is at its peak. A morning person hit more products, as it's said that sunrise is when you get active. Mostly from 8 o'clock to 10 o'clock. It's said that morning is the time when our minds work the sharpest. It provides you alertness and good memory ability. It is also called the "protected time." We get a new sense to think from, and then we get a sound vision of our steps and ideas to a routine of peak productivity.

Charles Duhigg is a known news reporter, works for the New York Times. He tells us to stop procrastinating and visualizing our next step in life. Not only does it give you confidence, but it also gives you a satisfactory feeling. You get an idea of the result, and you tend to do things more that way. This way, you get habitual of thinking about your next step beforehand. Habits are gradually formed. They are difficult to change but easy to assemble. A single practice can bring various elements from it. Those elements can help you learn the routine of an expert.

You will eventually fall into place. No one can change themselves in one day. Hard work is the key to any outcome. Productivity is the result of many factors but, an excellent daily routine is an integral part of it which we all need to follow. Once you fall into working constantly, you won't notice how productive you have become. It becomes a habit. There might be tough decisions along the way, which is typical for an average life. We need to focus on what's in front of us and start with giving attention to one single task on top of your priority list. That way, you can achieve more in less time. These are some factors and advice to start a daily routine for reaching the peak of productivity with the help of some great products.

Chapter 10:

Constraints Make You Better: Why the Right Limitations Boost Performance

It is not uncommon to complain about the constraints in your life. Some people say that they have little time, money, and resources, or their network is limited. Yes, some of these things can hold us back, but there is a positive side to all of this. These constraints are what forces us to make choices and cultivate talents that can otherwise go undeveloped. Constraints are what drives creativity and foster skill development. In many ways reaching the next level of performance is simply a matter of choosing the right constraints.

How to Choose the Right Constraints

There are three primary steps that you can follow when you are using constraints to improve your skills.

1. **Decide what specific skill you want to develop.**

The more specific you are in the skill, the easier it will be to design a good constraint for yourself. You shouldn't try to develop the skill of being "good at marketing," for example. It's too broad. Instead, focus on learning how to write compelling headlines or analyze website data—something specific and tangible.

2. Design a constraint that requires this specific skill to be used

There are three main options for designing a constraint: time, resources, and environment.

- **Time:** Give yourself less time to accomplish a task or set a schedule that forces you to work on skills more consistently.

- **Resources:** Give yourself fewer resources (or different resources) to do a task.

- **Environment:** According to one study, if you eat on 10-inch plates rather than 12-inch plates, you'll consume 22 percent fewer calories over a year. One simple change in the environment can lead to significant results. In my opinion, environmental constraints are best because they impact your behavior without you realizing it.

3. Play the game

Constraints can accelerate skill development, but they aren't a magic pill. You still need to put in your time. The best plan is useless without repeated action. What matters most is getting your reps in.

The idea is to practice, experiment with different constraints to boost your skills. As for myself, I am working on storytelling skills these days. I have some friends who are amazing storytellers. I've never been great at it, but I'd like to get better. The constraint I've placed on myself is scheduling talks without the use of slides. My last five speaking engagements have used no slides or a few basic images. Without text to rely on, I have designed a constraint that forces me to tell better stories so that I don't embarrass myself in front of the audience.

So, the question here is What do you want to become great at? What skills do you want to develop? Most importantly, what constraints can you place upon yourself to get there? Figure these things out and start from today!

Bounce Back From Failure

Failure is a big word. It is a negative word most say. It is cursed in most cases. It is frowned upon when it is on your plate. But why?

Sure, it certainly doesn't feel good when you encounter failure. We can't even forgive ourselves for failing at a simple card game. We get impatient, we get hopeless and ultimately we get depressed on even the smallest of failure we go through in everyday life.

Why is it that way? Why can't we try to change a failure into something better? Why can't we just leave that failure right there and not try to make a big deal out of each and every small little setback?

These questions have a very deep meaning and a very important place in everyone's life.

Let's start with the simplest step to make it easy for yourself to deal with a certain failure. Whenever you fail at anything, just pause for a second and talk to yourself.

Rewind what you just went through. Talk to yourself through the present circumstances. Think about what you could have done to improve at what you just did. Think about what you could have done to prevent whatever tragic incident you went through. Or what you could have done to do better at what you felt like failing at.

These questions will immediately sketch a scenario in front of your eyes. A scenario where you can actually see yourself flourishing and doing your best against all odds.

Whatever happened to you, I am sure you didn't deserve it. But so what if you

Lost some money or a loved one or your pet? Ask yourself this, is it the end of the world? Have you stopped breathing? Have you no reason left to keep living?

You had, you have, and you will always have a new thing, a new person a new place to start with. Life has endless possibilities for you to find. But you just have to bounce back from whatever setback you think you cannot get out of.

Take for example the biggest tech billionaires in the world. I am giving this example because people tend to relate more to these examples these days. Elon Musk started his carrier with a small office with his brother and they both lived in the same office for a whole year. They couldn't even afford a small place for themselves to rent.

There was a time when Elon had to decide to split his last set of investments between two companies. If he had invested in one, the other would have gone down for sure, just to give a chance to the other company to maybe become their one big hit. Guess what, he ended up keeping them both because he invested in both.

Why did he succeed? Was it because he wasn't afraid? No!

He succeeded because he had Faith after all the failures he had faced. He knew that if he kept trying against all odds and even the obvious risks, he will ultimately succeed at something for what he worked so hard for all this time!

PART 3

Chapter 1:

Believe in Yourself

Listen up. I want to tell you a story. This story is about a boy. A boy who became a man, despite all odds. You see, when he was a child, he didn't have a lot going for him. The smallest and weakest in his class, he had to struggle every day just to keep up with his peers. Every minute of every hour was a fight against an opponent bigger and stronger than he was - and every day he was knocked down. Beaten. Defeated. But... despite that... despite everything that was going against him... this small, weak boy had one thing that separated him from hundreds of millions of people in this world. A differentiating factor that made a difference in the matter of what makes a winner in this world of losers. You see this boy believed in himself. No matter the odds, he believed fundamentally that he had the power to overcome anything that got in his way! It didn't matter how many times he was knocked down, he got RIGHT BACK UP!

Now it wasn't easy. It hurt like hell. Every time he failed was another reminder of how far behind he was. A reminder of the nearly insurmountable gap between him and everyone else and lurking behind that reminder was the temptation, the suggestion to just give up. Throw in the towel. Surrender the win. Yet believe me when I tell you that no matter HOW tough things got, no matter HOW much he wanted to give in, a small voice in his heart keep saying… not today… just once more… I know it hurts but I can try again… Just. Once. More.

You see more than anything in this world HE KNEW that deep inside him was a greatness just WAITING to be tapped into! A power that most people would never see, but not him. It didn't matter what the world threw at him, because he'd be damned if he let his potential die alongside him. And all it took? All it required to unlock the chasm of greatness inside was a moment to realise the lies the world tried to tell him. In less than a second he recognised the light inside that would ignite a spark of success to address the ones who didn't believe that he could do it. The ones who told him to give up! Get out! Go home and roam the streets where failure meets those who weren't born to sit at the seat at the top!

Yet what they didn't know is that being born weak didn't matter any longer 'cause in his fight to succeed he became stronger. Rising up to the heights beyond, he WOULD NOT GIVE UP till he forged a bond within his heart that ensured NO MATTER THE ODDS, no matter what anyone said about him, no matter what the world told him, he had something that NO ONE could take away from him. A power so strong it transformed this boy into a man. A loser into a winner. A failure into a success. That, is the power of self-belief…

Chapter 2:
Happy People Only Focus on What Is Within Their Control

We cloud our judgment and lose the sense of our role in shaping our reality.

Such can be the case today.

We're fighting through a global pandemic, and I can assure you every one of us is having good days and bad days.

On the good days, we try to stay positive and be productive. On the bad days, we sulk into the worry of predicting what the future will be like. We imagine it, and then we start living it, which leaves us feeling helpless and scared.

Thoughts fire before emotions—that's why when we think negatively, we feel negative emotions.

But there's a way around this.

Whenever I find myself moving from a positive outlook to a negative one, I try my best to bring my attention back to the most important aspect of all.

I ask myself these three questions:

1. What is worrying me?
2. What is within my control?
3. What matters most to me, and what can I do about it?

When we focus on what we can control, our thoughts empower us and then trigger positive emotions.

Do we give our power away to factors we cannot control, or do we retain it and direct our energy onto the options we can control?

When my mind plays tricks on me and slides me into a stream of worry, I consciously try to swim out of it. And I use this framework below to reorient my thoughts and whisk them up into a more sunny state of mind.

A Sunshine State of Mind

At any given stage in your life, regardless of the set of circumstances you are dealing with, you can find yourself in one of four mental states:

- **Quadrant #1: Wasting your energy.** When you focus on what is not within your control, you're wasting your energy on factors that will not move you forward. This is like having a 2-week vacation booked, which was canceled due to the pandemic. You can complain all you want, but what's the use? Stop draining your energy on it and start thinking clearly.

- **Quadrant #2: Being paranoid.** When you ignore what is not within your control, you're paranoid. You shouldn't ignore external factors, instead, accept what is and be aware of the external conditions that are outside your control. For instance, with this pandemic, we must understand the situation and how it progresses because its advancements have implications on our lives. We don't want to give our undivided attention, but we do want to stay educated on it.

- **Quadrant #3: In a sunshine state of mind.** When you focus on what is within your control, you're in the driver's seat. You're intentional about your attitude and how you spend your energy. This is where you are emotionally mature and thinking rationally and clearly in a sunshine state of mind. And what does it do to you? It keeps you positive, energized, and motivated.

Chapter 3:
Happy People Live Slow

"Slow Living means **structuring your life around meaning and fulfilment**. Similar to 'voluntary simplicity and 'downshifting,' it emphasizes a **less-is-more approach**, focusing on the quality of your life…Slow Living addresses the desire to lead a more balanced life and pursue a **more holistic sense of well-being** in the fullest sense of the word. In addition to the personal advantages, there are potential **environmental benefits** as well. When we slow down, we often use fewer resources and produce less waste, both of which have a lighter impact on the earth."

Slow living is a state of mind that will make you feel purposeful and is more fulfilling. It is all about being consistent and steady. Now that you have an idea of slow living, we will break down some myths attached to slow living and how to start slow living for mind peace and happiness. The first myth is that slow living is about doing everything as slowly as possible. Slow living is not about doing everything in slow motion but doing things at the right speed and not rushing. It is all about gaining time so you can do things that are important to you. The second myth is that slow living is the same as simple living. Now simple living is more worldly, and simple living is more focused on time.

The third myth is that slow living is an aesthetic that you see on desaturated Instagram posts, but that is not true; this is considered a minimalist aesthetic, whereas slow living is a minimalist lifestyle. The 4th myth is that slow living is about doing and being less. That is not at all true. It is all about removing the non-essentials from your life so you can have more time to be yourself. And the last myth is that slow living is anti-technology now. This is not about travelling back in time but all about using tech as a tool and not vice versa.

If you like this idea of living, we are going to list ten ways in which you can start slow living;

1. Define what is most important to you(essentials)
2. Say no to everything else (non-essentials)
3. Understand busyness and that it is a choice
4. Create space and margin in your day and life
5. Practice being present
6. Commit to putting your life before work
7. Adopt a slow information diet
8. Get outside physically and connect dots mentally
9. Start slow and small by downshifting
10. Find inspiration in the slow living community

Sit back and think about what the purpose of your life is, what you ultimately want from your life and not just in a monetary sense. Think about what you would like for your lifestyle to be 50 years from now, and then start working on it today. Suppose you have not figured out the purpose. In that case, there are multiple personality tests available on the internet that will help you determine your personality type and then eventually help you create your purpose.

6 Steps To Focus On Growth

Growth is a lifelong process. We grow every moment from the day we are born until our eventual death. And the amazing thing about growth is that there is no real limit to it.

Now, what exactly is growth? Well, growing is the process of changing from one state to another and usually, it has to be positive; constructive; better-than-before. Although growth occurs equally towards all directions in the early years of our life, the rate of growth becomes more and more narrowed down to only a few particular aspects of our life as we become old. We become more distinctified as individuals, and due to our individuality, not everyone of us can possibly grow in all directions. With our individual personality, experiences, characteristics, our areas of growth become unique to us. Consequently, our chances of becoming successful in life corresponds to how we identify our areas of growth and beam them on to our activities with precision. Let us explore some ways to identify our key areas of growth and utilize them for the better of our life.

1. **Identify Where You Can Grow**

For a human being, growth is relative. One person cannot grow in every possible way because that's how humans are—we simply cannot do every thing at once. One person may grow in one way while another may grow in a completely different way. Areas of growth can be so unlike that one's positive growth might even seem like negative growth to another person's perspective. So, it is essential that we identify the prime areas where we need to grow. This can be done through taking surveys, asking people or critically analyzing oneself. Find out what lackings do you have as a human being, find out what others think that you lack as a human being. Do different things and note down where you are weak but you have to do it anyway. Then, make a list of those areas where you need growing and move on to the next step.

2. Accept That You Need To Grow In Certain Areas

After carefully identifying your lackings, accept these in your conscious and subconscious mind. Repeatedly admit to yourself and others that you lack so and so qualities where you wish to grow with time.

Never feel ashamed of your shortcomings. Embrace them comfortably because you cannot trully change yourself without accepting that you need to change. Growth is a dynamic change that drags you way out of your comfort zone and pushes you into the wild. And to start on this endeavor for growth, you need to have courage. Growth is a choice that requires acceptance and humility.

3. Remind Yourself of Your Shortcomings

You can either write it down and stick it on your fridge or just talk about it in front of people you've just met—this way, you'll constantly keep reminding yourself that you have to grow out of your lackings. And this remembrance will tell you to try—try improving little by little. Try growing.

It is important to remain consciously aware of these at all times because you never know when you might have to face what. All the little and big things you encounter every day are all opportunities of growth. This takes us to the fourth step:

4. Face Your Problems

Whatever you encounter, in any moment or place in your life is an opportunity created: an opportunity for learning. A very old adage goes: "the more we learn, the more we grow". So, if you don't face your problems and run away from them, then you are just losing the opportunity to learn from it, and thus, losing the opportunity of growing from it. Therefore, facing whatever life throws at you also has an important implication on your overall growth. Try to make yourself useful against all odds. Even if you fail at it, you will grow anyway.

5. Cross The Boundary

So, by now you have successfully identified your areas of growth, you have accepted them, you constantly try to remind yourself of them and you face everything that comes up, head on—never running away. You are already making progress. Now comes the step where you push yourself beyond your current status. You go out of what you are already facing and make yourself appear before even more unsettling circumstances.

This is a very difficult process, but if you grow out of here, nothing can stop you ever. And only a few people successfully make it through. You create your own problems, no one might support you and yet still, you try to push forward, make yourself overcome new heights of difficulties and grow like the tallest tree in the forest. You stand out of the crowd. This can only be done in one or two subjects in a lifetime. So make sure that you know where you want to grow. Where you want to invest that much effort, and time, and dedication. Then, give everything to it. Growth is a life's journey.

6. Embrace Your Growth

After you have crossed the boundary, there is no turning back. You have achieved new heights in your life, beyond what you thought you could have ever done. The area—the subject in which you tried to develop yourself, you have made yourself uniquely specialized in that particular area. You have outgrown the others in that field. It is time for you to make yourself habituated with that and embrace it gracefully. The wisdom you've accumulated through growth is invaluable—it has its roots deeply penetrated into your life. The journey that you've gone through while pursuing your growth will now define you. It is who you are.

As I've mentioned in the first line, "growth is a lifelong process". Growth is not a walk in the park, It is you tracking through rough terrains—steep heights and unexplored depths for an entire lifetime. Follow these simple yet difficult steps; grow into the tallest tree and your life will shine upon you like the graceful summer sun.

Chapter 4:
8 Ways To Deal With Setbacks In Life

Life is never the same for anyone - It is an ever-changing phenomenon, making you go through all sorts of highs and lows. And as good times are an intrinsic part of your life, so are bad times. One day you might find yourself indebted by 3-digit figures while having only $40 in your savings account. Next day, you might be vacationing in Hawaii because you got a job that you like and pays $100,000 a year. There's absolutely no certainty to life (except passing away) and that's the beauty of it. You never know what is in store for you. But you have to keep living to see it for yourself. Setbacks in life cannot be avoided by anyone. Life will give you hardships, troubles, break ups, diabetes, unpaid bills, stuck toilet and so much more. It's all a part of your life.

Here's 8 ways that you might want to take notes of, for whenever you may find yourself in a difficult position in dealing with setback in life.

1. **Accept and if possible, embrace it**

The difference between accepting and embracing is that when you accept something, you only believe it to be, whether you agree or disagree. But when you embrace something, you truly KNOW it to be true and accept it as a whole. There is no dilemma or disagreement after you have embraced something.

So, when you find yourself in a difficult situation in life, accept it for what it is and make yourself whole-heartedly believe that this problem in your life, at this specific time, is a part of your life. This problem is what makes you complete. This problem is meant for you and only you can go through it. And you will. Period. There can be no other way.

The sooner you embrace your problem, the sooner you can fix it. Trying to bypass it will only add upon your headaches.

2. **Learn from it**

Seriously, I can't emphasize how important it is to LEARN from the setbacks you face in your life. Every hardship is a learning opportunity. The more you face challenges, the more you grow. Your capabilities expand with every issue you solve—every difficulty you go through, you rediscover yourself. And when you finally deal off with it, you are reborn. You are a new person with more wisdom and experience.

When you fail at something, try to explore why you failed. Be open-minded about scrutinizing yourself. Why couldn't you overcome a certain situation? Why do you think of this scenario as a 'setback'? The moment you find the answers to these questions is the moment you will have found the solution.

3. Execute What You Have Learnt

The only next step from here is to execute that solution and make sure that the next time you face a similar situation, you'll deal with it by having both your arms tied back and blindfolded. All you have to do is remember what you did in a similar past experience and reapply your previous solution.

Thomas A. Edison, the inventor of the light bulb, failed 10,000 times before finally making it. And he said "I have not failed. I just found 10,000 ways that won't work".

The lesson here is that you have to take every setback as a lesson, that's it.

4. Without shadow, you can never appreciate light

This metaphor is applicable to all things opposite in this universe. Everything has a reciprocal; without one, the other cannot exist. Just as without shadow, we wouldn't have known what light is, similarly, without light, we could've never known about shadow. The two opposites identify and complete each other.

Too much of philosophy class, but to sum it up, your problems in life, ironically, is exactly why you can enjoy your life. For example, if you are a chess player, then defeating other chess players will give you enjoyment while getting defeated will give you distress. But, when you are a chess prodigy—you have defeated every single chess player on earth and there's no one else to defeat, then what will you do to derive pleasure? Truth is, you can now no longer enjoy chess. You have no one to defeat. No one gives you the fear of losing anymore and as a result, the taste of winning has lost its appeal to you.

So, whenever you face a problem in life, appreciate it because without it, you can't enjoy the state of not having a problem. Problems give you the pleasure of learning from them and solving them.

5. View Every Obstacle As an opportunity

This one's especially for long term hindrances to your regular life. The COVID-19 pandemic for instance, has set us back for almost two years now. As distressing it is, there is also some positive impact of it. A long-term setback opens up a plethora of new avenues for you to explore. You suddenly get a large amount of time to experiment with things that you have never tried before.

When you have to pause a regular part of your life, you can do other things in the meantime. I believe that every one of us has a specific talent and most people never know what their talent is simply because they have never tried that thing.

6. Don't Be Afraid to experiment

People pursue their whole life for a job that they don't like and most of them never ever get good at it. As a result, their true talent gets buried under their own efforts. Life just carries on with unfound potential. But when some obstacle comes up and frees you from the clutches of doing what you have been doing for a long time, then you should get around and experiment. Who knows? You, a bored high school teacher, might be a natural at tennis. You won't know it unless you are fired from that job and actually play tennis to get over it. So whenever life gives you lemons, quit trying to hold on to it. Move on and try new things instead.

7. Stop Comparing yourself to others

The thing is, we humans are emotional beings. We become emotionally vulnerable when we are going through something that isn't supposed to be. And in such times, when we see other people doing fantastic things in life, it naturally makes us succumb to more self-loathing. We think lowly of our own selves and it is perfectly normal to feel this way. Talking and comapring ourselves to people who are seemingly untouched by setbacks is a counterproductive move. You will listen to their success-stories and get depressed—lose self-esteem. Even if they try their best to advise you, it won't get through to you. You won't be able to relate to them.

8. **Talk to people other people who are having their own setbacks in life**

I'm not asking you to talk to just any people. I'm being very specific here: talk to people who are going through bad times as well.

If you start talking to others who are struggling in life, perhaps more so compared to you, then you'll see that everyone else is also having difficulties in life. It will seem natural to you. Moreover, having talked with others might even show you that you are actually doing better than all these other people. You can always find someone who is dealing with more trouble than you and that will enlighten you. That will encourage you. If someone else can deal with tougher setbacks in life, why can't you?

Besides, listening to other people will give you a completely new perspective that you can use for yourself if you ever find yourself in a similar situation as others whom you have talked with.

Conclusion

Setbacks are a part of life. Without them we wouldn't know what the good times are. Without them we wouldn't appreciate the success that we have gotten. Without them we wouldn't cherish the moments that got us to where we are heading to. And without them there wouldn't be any challenge to fill our souls with passion and fire. Take setbacks as a natural process in the journey. Use it to fuel your drive. Use it to move your life forward one step at a time.

Chapter 5:
Happy People Create Time to Do What They Love Every Day

Most of our days are filled with things that we need to do and the things we do to destress ourselves. But, in between all this, we never get time for things. We wanted to do things that bring us pure joy. So then the question is, When will we find time to do what we love? Then, when things calm down a bit and when the people who visit us leave or finish all the trips we have planned and wrap up our busy projects, and the kids will be grown, we will retire? Then, probably after we are dead, we will have more time.

You do not have to wait for things to get less busy or calmer. There will always be something coming up; trips, chores, visitors, errands, holidays, projects, death and illness. There is never going to be more time. Whatever you have been stuck in the past few years, it will always be like that. So now the challenge is not waiting for things to change it is to make time for things you love no matter how busy your life is. Sit down and think about what you want to do, something that you have been putting off. What is something that makes you feel fulfilled and happy? Everyone has those few things that make them fall in love with life think of what is that for you. If you haven't figured it out yet, we will give you some examples, and maybe you can try some of these things and see how that makes you feel.

- Communing with nature

- Going for a beautiful walk

- Creating or growing a business or an organization

- Hiking, running, biking, rowing, climbing

- Meditating, journaling, doing yoga, reflecting

- Communing with loved ones

- Crafting, hogging, blogging, logging, vlogging
- Reading aloud to kids
- Reading aloud to kids

Did you remember something you enjoyed doing, but as the responsibilities kept increasing, you sidelined it. Well, this is your sign to start doing what you loved to take time out for that activity every day, even if it is for 30 minutes only. Carve that time out for yourself, do it now. Once you start doing this, you will realize that you will have more energy because your brain will release serotonin, and your energy level will increase. Secondly, your confidence will improve because you will be making something love every day, and that will constantly help you gain confidence because you will be putting yourself in a happy, self-loving state. You will notice that you have started enjoying life more when you do something you love once a day. It makes the rest of your day brighter and happier. You will also want to constantly continue learning and growing because your brain will strive to do more and more of the thing you like to do, and that will eventually lead to an increased desire of learning and growing. Lastly, your motivation will soar because you will have something to look forward to that brings you pure joy.

Chapter 6:
Happy People Live Slow

"Slow Living means **structuring your life around meaning and fulfilment**. Similar to 'voluntary simplicity and 'downshifting,' it emphasizes a **less-is-more approach**, focusing on the quality of your life…Slow Living addresses the desire to lead a more balanced life and pursue a **more holistic sense of well-being** in the fullest sense of the word. In addition to the personal advantages, there are potential **environmental benefits** as well. When we slow down, we often use fewer resources and produce less waste, both of which have a lighter impact on the earth."

Slow living is a state of mind it will make you feel purposeful and is more fulfilling. It is all about being consistent and steady. Now that you have an idea of slow living, we will break down some myths attached to slow living and how to start slow living for mind peace and happiness. The first myth is that slow living is about doing everything as slowly as possible. Slow living is not about doing everything in slow motion but doing things at the right speed and not rushing. It is all about gaining time so you can do things that are important to you. The second myth is that slow living is the same as simple living. Now simple living is more worldly, and simple living is more focused on time.

The third myth is that slow living is an aesthetic that you see on desaturated Instagram posts, but that is not true; this is considered a minimalist aesthetic, whereas slow living is a minimalist lifestyle. The 4th myth is that slow living is about doing and being less. That is not at all true. It is all about removing the non-essentials from your life so you can have more time to be yourself. And the last myth is that slow living is anti-technology now. This is not about travelling back in time but all about using tech as a tool and not vice versa.

If you like this idea of living, we are going to list ten ways in which you can start slow living;

11. Define what is most important to you(essentials)
12. Say no to everything else (non-essentials)
13. Understand busyness and that it is a choice
14. Create space and margin in your day and life
15. Practice being present
16. Commit to putting your life before work
17. Adopt a slow information diet
18. Get outside physically and connect dots mentally
19. Start slow and small by downshifting
20. Find inspiration in the slow living community

Sit back and think about what the purpose of your life is, what you ultimately want from your life and not just in a monetary sense. Think about what you would like for your lifestyle to be 50 years from now, and then start working on it today. Suppose you have not figured out the purpose. In that case, there are multiple personality tests available on the internet that will help you determine your personality type and then eventually help you create your purpose.

Chapter 7:
7 Ways Your Behaviors Are Holding You Back

Habits and behaviors are what defines a human being and make you who you are. It is what shapes us and defines our lives while making us move towards our future. However, did you know that there are multiple things that hold you back?

These are the behavior that molds us, defines us, holds us back to be the better person and achieves everything that it takes to be perfect. Well, not that anyone is perfect; however, we all can aspire to be! Isn't it so? Let us explore and discuss the ways that your behaviors hold you back.

1. Not Accepting Your Faults

We have all been guilty of doing the same. Haven't we? I am so sure that each one of you has at least once committed this sin of shifting the blame to someone else and removing it off your shoulders. We are humans, after all; we are governed by our hearts, more than our minds. This is why we are more inclined to never accepting our faults instead of putting the blame on others.

Irrespective of the circumstance, it is necessary that you accept your fault, realize your weakness, and evaluate what needs to be done in order to never repeat the same. Going forward, you must find a way to turn your weakness into strength.

2. Having Self-Doubt

A lot of us are seen killing our dreams due to fear of being rejected. Haven't you already done the same a few times? Well, we all have! Self-doubt is one of the silent killers that can do you more harm than any good. If you constantly find yourself doubting your potential and stuck in a negative situation, you need to know that you are holding yourself back.

You can only look forward and attain a prosperous tomorrow when you stop doubting yourself. Self-doubt can be highly injurious, and this is one big reason why you need to stop holding yourself back and take a giant leap forward, or maybe a baby step! Shall we?

3. Procrastinating On Everything

No matter how many times we decide not to keep doing it, we keep doing it! Let's face it, and there are way too many distractions for us to procrastinate and sideline our current goals and duties. Say hello to social media! It distracts you way too many times than it should, especially when you are on the verge of serving your last-minute deadlines!

Hasn't it already got way too annoying? If it has, you must take a deep breath and train your mind. This is one of the behaviors that might hold you back. When you find yourself in such a situation, you must stop procrastinating; instead, do what you are supposed to do. Doing this will help you largely concentrate and uplift productivity.

4. Disrespecting Others

Do you often find yourself engaging in putting others down? If yes, then let me tell you that you are only inviting a lot of ill wrath for yourself. Imagine telling yourself that you are incapable, you are not good enough, and stuffs similar.

Similarly, if you do the same things to others, you are dragging everyone down. This is why you must stop being the harsh person that you are being and put your negativity aside. Disrespecting others or putting others down will only do more harm to you and your mental well-being. Why not focus more on what you can do to uplift others, encourage others and bring in more positivity around yourself!

5. Being In Your Cozy Corner

Not literally, but what we mean is you being in your own comfort zone! We all need our own comfort zones to feel safe and secured! But did you know that this is one such habit that holds you back? Yes, it holds you back from achieving a lot many things that you have only dreamt of. When you stay in your own comfort zone, you will never know what you are capable of.

Hence, unless and until you try your hands on something and step out of your comfort zone, you will never know what you are truly capable of.

Did you know that the brawny in the business, such as Bill Gates, Warren Buffet, and many other personalities, have all failed in life, at some point or the other! But what would have happened if they would have feared their failure and stayed in their comfort zone for the rest of their lives? Remember, with the risk comes to the possibility of achieving a reward. Hence, why hold yourself back and stay in your comfort zone when you can explore, wander and try everything that comes your way to know what you are capable of! Imagine what a great learning experience it will be!

6. Waiting For The Right Moment

Do you really think that there is a right moment for everything? If there were, then the law of gravity would not have been discovered, neither would we have received more significant innovations in life. Well, it is up to you to choose a moment and act! Yes, it is as simple as that!

If you keep living your life wandering about the right moment that will control your life and that you have your own sweet time to do everything, you will only lose on your precious time. Instead, we all must be accountable for our actions each day and grab the opportunity to try, create, explore, invent, experiment, and a lot more!

7. The Image of Being Perfect

Don't we feel that everyone around us is living their perfect lives? Sorry to burst your bubble, it is not so! Thanks to social media, we are always misguided to believe that others live their fairytales while we are sulking in our own lives! This is when we keep pushing ourselves to live a perfect life, be a perfect person and make everyone around us perfect!

But is it practically possible to do so? In fact, with doing so, we tend to set an unrealistic expectation and tends to harm our mental well being and relationships around us. Life is about swinging in the right direction at times, and sometimes in the opposite! Each of these scenarios brings with it its fruits, which must be graced with positivity.

Hence, let me tell you, there is no need for you to be perfect! Be however you are, but be your best version!

Conclusion:

Hence, kill these behaviors that hold you back. Instead, break the barrier and strive for a rewarding tomorrow. Let's try being a little different than we are? What say?

Chapter 8:

8 Habits That Can Make You Happy

We're always striving for something, whether it's a promotion, a new truck, or anything else. This brings us to an assumption that "when this happens, You'll finally be happy."

While these important events ultimately make us happy, research suggests that this pleasure does not last. A Northwestern University study compared the happiness levels of ordinary people to those who had won the massive lottery in the previous years. It was found that the happiness scores of both groups were nearly equal.

The false belief that significant life events determine your happiness or sorrow is so widespread that psychologists have given it a name- "impact bias." The truth is that event-based happiness is transitory. Satisfaction is artificial; either create it or not. Long-term happiness is achieved through several habits. Happy people develop behaviors that keep them satisfied daily.

Here are eight habits that can make you happy.

1. Take Pride in Life's Little Pleasures.

We are prone to falling into routines by nature. This is, in some ways, a positive thing. It helps conserve brainpower while also providing comfort. However, it is possible to be so engrossed in your routine that you neglect to enjoy the little pleasures in life. Happy people understand the value of savoring the taste of their meal, revel in a great discussion they just had, or even simply stepping outside to take a big breath of fresh air.

2. Make Efforts To Be Happy.

Nobody, not even the most ecstatically happy people, wakes up every day feeling this way. They work harder than everyone else. They understand how easy it is to fall into a routine where you don't check your emotions or actively strive to be happy and optimistic. People who are happy continually assess their moods and make decisions with their happiness in mind.

3. Help other people.

Helping others not only makes them happy, but it also makes you happy. Helping others creates a surge of dopamine, oxytocin, and serotonin, all of which generate pleasant sensations. According to Harvard research, people who assist others are ten times more likely to be focused at work and 40% more likely to be promoted. According to the same study, individuals who constantly provide social support are the most likely to be happy during stressful situations. As long as you don't overcommit yourself, helping others will positively affect your mood.

4. Have Deep Conversations.

Happy people understand that happiness and substance go hand in hand. They avoid gossip, trivial conversation, and passing judgment on others. Instead, they emphasize meaningful interactions. You should interact with others on a deeper level because it makes you feel good, creates emotional connections, and, importantly, it's an intriguing way to learn.

5. Get Enough Sleep.

I've pounded this one too hard over the years, and I can't emphasize enough how important sleep is for enhancing your attitude, focus, and self-control. When you sleep, your brain recharges, removing harmful proteins that accumulate as byproducts of regular neuronal activity during the day. This guarantees that you awaken alert and focused. When you don't get enough quality sleep, your energy, attention, and memory all suffer. Even in the absence of a stressor, sleep loss elevates stress hormone levels. Sleep is vital to happy individuals because it makes them feel good, and they know how bad they feel when they don't get enough sleep.

6. Surround yourself with the right people

Happiness is contagious; it spreads through people. Surrounding yourself with happy people boosts your confidence, encourages your creativity, and is simply enjoyable. Spending time with negative people has the opposite effect. They get others to join their self-pity party so that they may feel better about themselves. Consider this: if someone was smoking, would you sit there all afternoon inhaling the second-hand smoke? You'd step back, and you should do the same with negative people.

7. Always Stay Positive.

Everyone, even happy people, encounters difficulties daily. Instead of moaning about how things could or should have been, happy people think about what they are grateful for. Then they find the best approach to the situation, that is, dealing with it and moving on. Pessimism is a powerful source of sadness. Aside from the damaging effects on your mood, the problem with a pessimistic mindset is that it becomes a self-fulfilling prophecy. If you expect bad things, you are more likely to encounter horrific events. Gloomy thoughts are difficult to overcome unless you see how illogical they are. If you force yourself to look at the facts, you'll discover that things aren't nearly as awful as you think.

8. Maintain a Growth Mindset.

People's core attitudes can be classified into two types: fixed mindsets and growth mindsets. You believe you are who you are and cannot change if you have a fixed attitude. When you are challenged, this causes problems because anything that looks to be more than you can handle will make you feel despondent and overwhelmed. People with a growth mindset believe that with effort, they can progress. They are happy as a result of their improved ability to deal with adversity. They also outperform those with a fixed perspective because they welcome difficulties and see them as chances to learn something new.

Conclusion

It can be tough to maintain happiness, but investing your energy in good habits will pay off. Adopting even a couple of the habits on this list will have a significant impact on your mood.

Chapter 9:

7 Ways To Attract Happiness

We have seen a lot of people defining success as to their best of knowledge. While happiness is subjective from person to person, there's a law of attraction that remains constant for everyone in the world. It states that you will indirectly start to attract all the good things in life when you become happier. This is why happy people often have good lives where everything just somehow tends to work for them. Happiness not only feels good but can also make our manifestation attempts twice as effective. We shouldn't measure our happiness from external factors but instead, as cliche as it may sound, we should know that true happiness comes from the inside.

Here are some ways for you to attract happiness:

1. **Make a choice to be happy:**

When you choose to be as happy as you can in every moment of your life, your subconscious mind will start acknowledging your decision, and it will begin to find ways to bring more joy into your life. When you work towards your decision of being happy, the universe also plays its part and makes sure it attracts more situations in your life that you can be pleased about. The positive vibrations that you will give out will find their way back to you. You don't have to make the decision of being happy right away, as some of you might be going through a tough time. Sit, relax, and take some time to reflect on yourself first and then make a choice whenever you're ready.

2. Define What Happiness Means To You

We have also found ourselves asking this question a million times, "what exactly is happiness?" Some people would attach the idea of happiness with materialistic things such as a big house, expensive cars, branded clothes and shoes, designer bags, the latest technologies, and so forth. While for some, happiness is merely spending time with family and friends, doing the things that they love, and finding inner peace and calm.

3. React Positively under all situations:

We could experience a thousand good things but a million bad ones in our everyday lives. And sometimes, it could be complicated for us to encounter any kind of happiness given the circumstances. Although these circumstances cannot be in our control, how we react to them is always in our hands. As our favorite Professor Dumbledore once said, "Happiness can be found even in the darkest of times if only one remembers to turn on the light." Similarly, we should always try to find that silver lining at the end of the dark tunnel, always seek some positivity in every situation. But we are only humans. Don't try to enforce positivity on yourself if you don't feel like it. It's okay to address all our emotions equally till you be yourself again.

4. **Do not procrastinate:**

You might find it a bit weird, but procrastination does snatch your happiness away. No matter how much things are going well in your life, you would always find a loophole, a reason to be unhappy and dissatisfy with yourself a well as your life. Procrastination makes you believe that you are not living up to your fullest potential. You will get this nagging feeling that will eventually morph into negative emotions that would nearly eat you. So, try to avoid procrastination as much as possible and start doing the things that actually matter.

5. **Stay present:**

The key to becoming more focused, more at peace, more effective in manifesting, and eventually, much happier is to just live in the moment. Whatever you're doing in the present, try to be completely aware and focused on it. It will help you avoid all the negative feelings you have conjured up about the past and future. Try to stay present as much as you can; over time, it will become a habit, and you will develop the capability to face it all. This will definitely help you attract more happiness into your life.

6. **Do not compare yourself:**

As Theodore Rosevelt once said, "Comparison is the thief of joy." Whenever we compare ourselves to others, we tend to become ungrateful and strip ourselves of the ability to appreciate the good and abundance in our lives. We start to magnify the good in other people's lives and the bad that is in our own. We must understand that everyone is going through their own pace, and they all are secretly struggling with one thing or the other.

7. Don't try too hard:

Happiness demands patience. It is better to get into it gradually rather than being overeager. Many people take the law of attraction and being positive a little too far and start obsessing over it. They tend to panic if they get negative thoughts or are unable to attract the things they want. Don't get frustrated if things don't work out your way, and don't give up on the idea of happiness if you feel distressed. Try to prioritize your happiness and give others a reason to be happy too. Make yours as well as other's lives easy.

Conclusion:

Not many people know that, but being happy is actually the foundation towards attracting all your dreams and goals. When you adopt the habit of becoming truly happy every day, everything good will naturally follow you. Over time, happiness can even become your default state. Try your best to follow the guidelines above, and I guarantee that you will start feeling happier immediately.

Chapter 10:
7 Ways To Cultivate Emotions That Will Lead You To Greatness

Billions of men and women have walked the earth but only a handful have made their names engraved in history forever. These handful of people have achieved 'greatness' owing to their outstanding work, their passion and their character.

Now, greatness doesn't come overnight—greatness is not something you can just reach out and grab. Greatness is the result of how you have lived your entire life and what you have achieved in your lifetime. Against all your given circumstances, how impactful your life has been in this world, how much value you have given to the people around you, how much difference your presence has made in history counts towards how great you are. However, even though human greatness is subjective, people who are different and who have stood out from everyone else in a particular matter are perceived as great.

However, cultivating greatness in life asks for a 'great' deal of effort and all kinds of human effort are influenced by human emotions. So it's safe to say that greatness is, in fact, controlled by our emotions. Having said that, let's see what emotions are associated with greatness and how to cultivate them in real life:

1. Foster Gratitude

You cannot commence your journey towards greatness without being grateful first. That's right, being satisfied with what you already have in life and expressing due gratitude towards it will be your first step towards greatness. Being in a gratified emotional state at most times (if not all) will enhance your mental stability which will consequently help you perceive life in a different—or better point of view. This enhanced perception of life will remove your stresses and allow you to develop beyond the mediocrity of life and towards greatness.

2. Be As Curious As Child

Childhood is the time when a person starts to learn whatever that is around them. A child never stops questioning, a child never runs away from what they have to face. They just deal with things head on. Such kind of eagerness for life is something that most of us lose at the expense of time. As we grow up—as we know more, our interest keeps diminishing. We stop questioning anymore and accept what is. Eventually, we become entrapped into the ordinary. On the contrary, if we greet everything in life with bold eagerness, we expose ourselves to opportunities. And opportunities lead to greatness.

3. Ignite Your Passion

Passion has become a cliché term in any discussion related to achievements and life. Nevertheless, there is no way of denying the role of passion in driving your life force. Your ultimate zeal and fervor towards what you want in life is what distinguishes you to be great. Because admittedly, many people may want the same thing in life but how bad they want it—the intensity of wanting something is what drives people to stand out from the rest and win it over.

4. Become As Persistent As A Mountain

There are two types of great people on earth—1) Those who are born great and 2) Those who persistently work hard to become great. If you're reading this article, you probably belong to the later criteria. Being such, your determination is a key factor towards becoming great. Let nothing obstruct you—remain as firm as a mountain through all thick and thin. That kind of determination is what makes extraordinary out of the ordinary.

5. Develop Adaptability

As I have mentioned earlier, unless you are born great, your journey towards greatness will be an extremely demanding one. You will have to embrace great lengths beyond your comfort. In order to come out successful in such a journey, make sure that you become flexible to unexpected changes in your surroundings. Again, making yourself adaptable first in another journey in itself. You can't make yourself fit in adverse situations immediately. Adaptability or flexibility is cultivated prudently, with time, exposing yourself to adversities, little by little.

6. Confidence Is Key

Road to greatness often means that you have to tread a path that is discouraged by most. It's obvious—by definition, everybody cannot be great. People will most likely advise against you when you aspire something out of the ordinary. Some will even present logical explanations against you;especially your close ones. But nothing should waver your faith. You must remain boldly confident towards what you're pursuing. Only you can bring your greatness. Believe that.

7. Sense of Fulfilment Through Contributions

Honestly, there can be no greater feeling than what you'd feel after your presence has made a real impact on this world. If not, what else do we live for? Having contributed to the world and the people around you; this is the purpose of life. All the big and small contributions you make give meaning to your existence. It connects you to others, man and animal alike. It fulfills your purpose as a human being. We live for this sense of fulfillment and so, become a serial contributor. Create in yourself a greed for this feeling. At the end of the day, those who benefit from your contributions will revere you as great. No amount of success can be compared with this kind of greatness. So, never miss the opportunity of doing a good deed, no matter how minuscule or enormous.

In conclusion, these emotions don't come spontaneously. You have to create these emotions, cultivate them. And to cultivate these emotions, you must first understand yourself and your goals. With your eye on the prize, you have to create these emotions in you which will pave the path to your greatness. Gratitude, curiosity, passion, persistence, adaptability and fulfillment—each has its own weight and with all the emotions at play, nothing can stop you from becoming great in the truest form.

www.ingramcontent.com/pod-product-compliance
Lightning Source LLC
LaVergne TN
LVHW010342070526
838199LV00065B/5769